Sometimes I Hurt

Sometimes I Hurt

Reflections on the Book of Job

Mildred Tengbom

Publishing House
St. Louis

Cover: Ed Cooper Photo

Copyright © 1986 by Concordia Publishing House
3558 South Jefferson Avenue, St. Louis, MO 63118-3968
Manufactured in the United States of America

Library of Congress Cataloging-in-Publication Data

Tengbom, Mildred.
    Sometimes I hurt.

    1. Bible. O.T. Job—Meditations. 2. Consolation.
3. Tengbom, Mildred. I. Title.
BS1415.4.T46 1986   223'.106   85-16830
ISBN 0-570-03981-9 (pbk.)

1 2 3 4 5 6 7 8 9 10 PP 95 94 93 92 91 90 89 88 87 86

This book is lovingly dedicated to Pastor Rudolph C. Burke, who gently led me, when I was 15 years of age, to assurance of salvation and a personal encounter with Jesus Christ, my Savior and Lord, to whom I owe everything.

We have much to learn as the children of God.
The most difficult, perhaps, is to learn
        how to regard our trials and tribulations
        even the tragedies that beset us
        as capable of enhancing and enriching our lives.
Whereas God does not send them, He does permit them,
        and He can use them to draw us closer to Him
        and thereby accomplish His purposes
        in and through us.
We desperately need the wisdom to accept these
        painful happenings with graciousness, even with joy,
        knowing that whatever they may be,
        God can transform them from ugliness into beauty,
        from the plots of Satan designed to destroy
        into the purposes of God
        destined to do us good.
The key is genuine faith in a loving God,
        a faith that frees us and strengthens us
        to endure whatever may come our way.*

—Leslie Brandt, *Epistles/Now*
    JAMES I

_____
        *From EPISTLES/NOW by Leslie F. Brandt
© 1977 Concordia Publishing House.

He is the most wretched of people who has never felt adversity. Sweet are the uses of adversity, which, like the toad, ugly and venomous, wears yet a precious jewel in his head.

—Shakespeare

Sometimes I Hurt

Sometimes I hurt.
Sometimes—thank God, not always.

In fact, looking back over my life, I must acknowledge that God has presented me with far more joy-filled days than sad ones. And yet I find myself deeply grateful for the difficult, sorrow-drenched days, perhaps even more than for the easy, happy days. For difficult days have enriched my spirit so much that I find myself singing with the hymn writer, Adelaide Anne Procter:

> "I thank you, Lord that all my joy
> Is touched with pain.
> That shadows fall on brightest hours
> That thorns remain,
> So that earth's bliss may be my guide
> And not my chain."

It was a personal quest that led me to the Book of Job.

Thirty-two years ago at Easter I gave birth prematurely to a son. He gasped through eight hours and then died. A year later, again at Easter, I gave birth to a second son, again prematurely. This little son also lived about eight hours and then died.

In order for you to better understand why these bereavements were such a profound disappointment, let me retrace some of my life.

My marriage came as a delayed answer to prayer. When, at 16, I began to sense God was calling me to serve Him overseas, I shared this with an older missionary on leave in the States.

"Great!" he said enthusiastically, slipping his arm around my shoulder. "Pray that God will give you a husband so you can go together." No teen-ager would protest this romantic bit of advice, and since my father, too, thought it excellent counsel, I began to pray.

After a while I reasoned, "If I really believe God will answer my prayer, my future husband must be living now." So I began to intercede for him. But no husband appeared.

Then one summer night in northern Minnesota, as I was sitting on a pier that jutted out into a lake, God began to deal with me. The scene is still vivid: an electrical storm building up; dark clouds racing; wind blowing ominously; lightning ripping the sky; the low, threatening rumble of distant thunder; waves lapping against the pier.

"I want you to go to the Nepal border alone," God was saying.

Confused, I questioned, "But where is my husband?"

But the answer was always the same, "I want you to go alone."

I drew up my knees, wrapped my arms around them, rested my chin on my knees, and tried to pray. I struggled and struggled. At last God enabled me to say a tearful yes. Suddenly I was free and at peace. I jumped up, stretched out my arms as though to embrace the approaching storm, and ran back to our cabin just as the first drops of rain pelted down.

I went to India alone and spent seven of the most gloriously happy years of my life among the Nepali people, convinced I was where God wanted me. And I made the added welcome discovery that I could be single and happy, single and a whole person.

After seven years I returned to the United States on leave, and there, through an extraordinary set of circumstances, I met Luverne. Love sparked immediately. We discovered that our goals and aspirations, our likes and dislikes were marvellously in harmony. After much prayer, we were convinced God wanted us to join our lives together.

So it was that after years of praying for a husband and then finding joy in God's seeming denial of my request, my prayer was answered. I marvelled. And when God called Luverne overseas to East Africa, my cup of joy spilled over.

But to be honest, the death of our little sons dropped bitterness into our overflowing cup of joy. The first death caught me unawares. But I was prepared to fight for the life of our second baby, and fight I did. I prayed that God would heal the baby's immature lungs and enable him to live. I declared my faith to our doctor when he came into my room (in those days we were told if we believed we should "declare our faith"). With infinite pity our doctor looked at me and said, "Mrs. Tengbom, your baby is already dead."

With those words my faith in God began to tumble and dive like an airplane out of control. And crash it did!

What a variety of emotions captured me! Despair. Resentment. Hurt. The feelings that God had disappointed me. Confusion. Depression. Questionings. Doubt. Guilt—lots of guilt. I thought I had not "believed enough"; or perhaps I had not taken all the possible precautions during my pregnancy. Feelings of inadequacy. Failure. Bruised self-esteem. But most of all, I felt deep anger within.

I felt God was not just. *Luverne and I would make good parents, would we not?* I asked myself. We loved children. We would seek to bring them up in the fear and love of God. We had waited so long to get married, and now this? What about all those who thoughtlessly conceived children and then did away with them? Was it fair of God to let our children die while others were allowed to kill theirs? Or what of the unwanted babies born into homes where they would be mistreated?

Hadn't we sought to walk in obedience to God? What made Him think He could treat us in this way now? On and on the anger raged, deep and terrible. It was also destructive, because at that time I didn't know the necessity of getting my anger out in the open and looking at it for what it was. Depression resulted, and although I skillfully hid it, it left me numb, feeling I could never ask God for anything again.

Recovery and healing finally did come—slowly, very slowly. But the hurt had been deep and grievous.

Many years later, another difficult experience came, and I found my anger boiling again. It was then that I prayerfully determined to let the Holy Spirit probe and examine me to see if vestiges of my previous anger still lingered within my heart. I turned to God and asked Him to search my heart.

He led me into the Book of Job. There I gained insight into many of my reactions. As I lived in the book week after week and month after month, joining Job in his search, a new healing took place. God became more dear to me, and I was enabled to trust Him for things I couldn't before. Awe and wonder captivated me afresh, and I had a renewed desire to be wholly His.

I began to better understand the experience of George Matheson, one of Scotland's ablest preachers in the 1880s and a world-renowned writer of devotional literature. He had become blind soon after he entered the University of Glasgow. In spite of this, he graduated at 19. At 26, he took over his first parish. When he was 44, the large St. Bernard Parish Church in Edinburgh called him to be its pastor. A gracious, warm person, he was loved by thousands. One of his recorded prayers now took on deeper meaning for me.

O Divine Spirit,
who in all the events of life are knocking at the door of
    my heart,
help me to respond to Thee.
I would take the events of my life as good and
    perfect gifts from Thee.
I would receive even the sorrows of life as disguised gifts
    from Thee.
I would have my heart open at all times to receive;
    at morning, noon, and night,
      in spring and summer and winter.
Whether Thou comest to me in sunshine or in rain,
    I would take Thee into my heart joyfully.
Thou art Thyself more than sunshine;
Thou art Thyself compensation for the rain.
It is Thee, and not Thy gifts, I crave.
Knock, and I shall open unto Thee.

This, then, was my personal reason for exploring the Book of Job. In the pages that follow, I will share some of my insights. I do so with the prayer that, if you have been searching, you may gain understanding that will help you in your relationship with God and draw you closer to Him. He loves you.

How Can I Understand the Book of Job?

Before we get into the Book of Job, I would like to share a few facts with you. I hope you will read this chapter carefully, because it will help you grasp the entire Book of Job.

May I suggest that you do your Bible reading in Today's English Version, or as we commonly know it *The Good News Bible*. The translation is clear. A second choice would be the New International Version.

Wisdom Literature

The Book of Job is perhaps the oldest book in the Bible. Scholars classify it as "wisdom literature," which possesses certain characteristics.

1. The message is vigorously practical and designed to help with everyday problems.

2. The insights and understanding portrayed are not colored or determined by the cultural, social, or economic position of the people of that day. Therefore, even today a

poor Christian in India can receive as much help from the Book of Job as an affluent, well-taught Christian in America (maybe more!).

3. The message is universal. Figures from nature are used for illustrations. For example: "My life passes . . . as fast as an eagle swooping down on a rabbit" (9:26).*

Poetry

A major portion of the Book of Job is poetry and should be understood as such. Parallelism characterizes Hebrew poetry—the same thought may be repeated in two ways. For example, we read: "Why won't God give me what I ask?" and then, immediately: "Why won't He answer my prayer?" (6:8). Hebrew poetry is also nontechnical and rich in figures and symbols that we should not take literally.

Drama

It was easier for me to understand the Book of Job when I viewed it as a drama. I visualized the play broken up into different scenes. Notice that the sixth scene is by far the most lengthy, containing the three sets of dialogue between Job and his friends.

Scene I (1:1-5)
Setting: Job's compound.
Characters: Job, his seven sons and three daughters.

Scene II (1:6-12)
Setting: The heavenly places.
Characters: The Lord and Satan.

---

*Unless otherwise indicated, all Bible references are from the Book of Job.

13

Scene III (1:13-22)
Setting: Job's compound.
Characters: Job and four messengers.

Scene IV (2:1-6)
Setting: Heavenly places.
Characters: The Lord and Satan.
(This scene is similar to Scene II and will not be discussed any further.)

Scene V (2:7-10)
Setting: The garbage dump.
Characters: Satan, Job, and Job's wife.

Scene VI (2:11—27:23)
Setting: Probably still the dump.
Characters: Job and his three friends: Eliphaz, Bildad, and Zophar.

Intermission (Job 28)

Scene VII (29:1—37:24)
Setting: Not stated.
Characters: Job and another friend, Elihu.

Scene VIII (38:1— 42:6)
Setting: Out-of-doors.
Characters: God and Job.

Scene IX (42:7-16)
Setting: Job's new home.
Characters: The Lord, Job, Eliphaz, Bildad, Zophar, and Job's family.

The drama has two kinds of characters: *hidden* and *apparent*. The chief hidden character is God. The opposing

14

hidden character is the devil. The issues are: Will Job continue to trust God when he experiences nothing but trouble? Will Job love God just for Himself when he receives no blessing or benefits from the relationship? Will Job trust God when He becomes the silent, inscrutable God? Will Job be able to declare, as Francis Xavier did:

How can I choose but love thee, God's dear Son,
O Jesus, lovliest and most loving One!
Were there no heav'n to gain, no hell to flee,
For what thou art alone I must love thee.

The apparent characters are Job, as chief character, and his wife. His four friends are opposing characters. Conflict ensues and grows intense between Job and his friends, because Job's friends insist he must have done something sinful to have brought this trouble on himself. Job refutes this. He does not claim to be sinless, but he insists that he knows of no particular sin he has committed that would merit this punishment. He repeatedly affirms his blamelessness and his desire to walk uprightly with his God.

Conflict arises between Job and the Lord, because Job cannot understand how God can be merciful and just and loving and allow this to happen to him. The Lord permits Job to voice his doubts, anger, resentments, and anguish, but He remains silent until the very end. Then He reveals Himself to Job. Faith is tested by darkness, doubt, and the silence of God; but it would never survive, blossom, or grow stronger without God's revelation of Himself. Both night and dawn are necessary, both questioning and revelation.

A Variety of Viewpoints Are Presented

We who are the readers or observers of this drama are omniscient viewers; we see what is going on from a number of viewpoints. We know what Satan's interest in the en-

15

counter is. We know God's viewpoint. We watch Job, who is ignorant of the tête-à-tête between Satan and God, struggling to work his way through a grief experience that has badly shaken his faith in a just and loving God. We see him withstanding the pressure brought to bear on him by his friends as they insinuate, accuse, intimidate, promise rewards, and use threats to get him to confess to some particular wrongdoing that Job knows he is not guilty of. And we see Job's friends—in their bumbling, self-righteous, smug, and mistaken way—trying to set right a friend who they think is behaving and talking in an unseemly and disturbing fashion for a child of God.

While the Book of Job does contain a grief experience, it does not present a picture of a man methodically working his way through clearly defined stages of grief. Rather, it is an account of confused people, of faith and doubt, of hope and despair, of anger and acceptance, of rebellion and surrender, of threats and promises. The characters skitter up and down on an emotional roller coaster. Often, one emotion has scarcely subsided before another moves in. Conversation is disjointed; threads of thought are continually broken; truth and error are confusedly intertwined.

But this very confusion authenticates the experience, portraying intense and sudden shock. Job's most prized possession—if we may call it that—his faith in God, is being threatened. When anyone is threatened with the loss of a loved one (in Job's case, his God)—and especially if that one has brought security—one's hope becomes a wild, primitive animal, clawing at anything that suggests our life together will not end. Unreasoning, passionate, and demanding, hope grows fierce and aggressive in desperate situations. Emotions and reactions are explosive, unpredictable, and sometimes unreasonable.

We find all these characteristics in the Book of Job. Once we understand that the confusion of the book is typical of experiences of severe loss and threatened security, we

16

shall be able to better unravel the puzzle and trace our way through the labyrinth of often unrelated and distracted thoughts.

I have found it helpful also to understand that there is both truth and error in what Job's friends say to him. Until we discern this, we too shall be confused—which, of course, was one of the results Satan hoped to achieve. As we move along through the book, we would do well to remember Satan's interest and participation in all that is happening. As Christians we *are* caught in a conflict between God and Satan.

If you are one who has suffered, that very suffering will equip you in a special way to gain insight and understanding from the struggles of our dear brother in the faith, Mr. Job.

Scene I
Job's Compound

Job, chief character: devout, upright, wealthy, probably middle-aged, a family man, warm in his family relationships.

Job's seven sons: of varying ages, wealthy, sociable, friendly, devoted to family.

Job's three daughters: beautiful, intelligent.

Reference: 1:1-5.

God created man a personal being, a partner in a dialogue, a being to whom he might speak and who could answer, to whom he gave liberty, and whose liberty, refusals and silences he respects, but whose replies he also awaits.

—Paul Tournier

He Knows Me by Name

There was a man named Job (1:1).

We must begin here. God knows His people by name.

God is not some impersonal power who created the universe and holds it in place and, being absorbed with these weighty responsibilities, has left humans on earth to fend for themselves. No, a thousand times, no!

The Bible, in its eagerness that humans understand God aright, spills over with declaration after declaration that God is a caring, loving God. He is a God who knows every earth creature by name and who makes Himself known through His incarnate Son, our Lord Jesus Christ.

"If that thought staggers you," Jesus said, in effect, one day to his students, "then what would you think if I told you God notes every time a wounded or old sparrow falls to the ground and dies? Now, no matter how low your self-esteem may be, you know you are of more value than a sparrow. So if God notices what is happening to birds, don't you think He notices what is happening to you? And not only does He notice, He cares."

God knows each of us by name.

"Fear not, for I have redeemed you; I have called you by name, you are mine," He declares (Is. 43:1, RSV).

When God broke into history by choosing to come to earth as a man, He demonstrated His personal, intimate interest in individuals. Jesus called His disciples by name.

And this personal relationship of being known to Him by name continues forever. Jesus said our names are recorded in heaven (Luke 10:20).

What would it mean to you if you read, "Go tell *(insert your name)* that Jesus is risen"? Think about it for a moment.

No, God is no impersonal God dwelling afar off, only now and again looking down His nose rather superciliously and pityingly at humans. Rather, He is tied up in the lives of all His earth creatures, loving them, hurting with them, seeking them, eager to help them, and most of all, longing for their loving, personal response.

My brain, magnificent as it is in its workings, cannot comprehend this. These thoughts stagger me. But if they did not, God would not be God, and I would not be human.

That does not mean that I do not still seek to understand and love God with my mind. But it means that when I reach my mental limits, I allow my heart to take over. For if I will listen closely to and follow my heart, it whispers to me that God does love me. He does care about me. And my heart further affirms that I need Him, that I am lonely because I am not joined to Him, and that I shall never be really, really at rest until I am. "The hungers of the heart outrun the reaches of the mind," Gerhard E. Frost affirms in *The Colors of the Night.*

If I am having difficulty believing this because my sophisticated, educated brain is getting in the way, I may ask God humbly to reveal this truth to me. He most surely will, and I shall stand in awe and wonder that in God's sight and awareness, I, Millie Tengbom (and you may insert your own name here), exist and God cares about me.

21

Without this basic understanding that God knows me by name and cares about me, the story that follows would be stripped of its most important meaning.

"There was a man named Job."

Discipleship means allegiance to the suffering
Christ, and it is therefore not at all surprising that
Christians should be called upon to suffer.
— Dietrich Bonhoeffer

Christians Suffer Too

A respected Christian leader wakes up one morning to hear
his wife of 15 years tell him she wants a divorce so she can
"live my own life" and "become my own person." Or a
faithful Christian wife is dumbfounded when her Christian
husband announces calmly that he "feels led of the Lord"
to leave her and marry another person to whom he feels
"God is guiding me." A God-fearing doctor trembles when
the police telephone him, saying they are holding his son,
who is charged with selling drugs. A godly farm couple weep
as their unwed daughter tells them she is pregnant. Another
couple listen, disbelieving, as their son admits he has been
living for months, unmarried, with a girl. A distinguished
professor at a seminary is crushed when his daughter joins
a revolutionary group and dies in a police shoot-out.

A bolt of lightning sets a barn ablaze, trapping a herd
of cattle inside. Cancer invades the body. A swollen river
swirls through a house, leaving a sediment of mud and silt.

And so suffering comes. Sometimes we bring it on ourselves. Sometimes others bring it on us. But sometimes,
through no apparent fault of ours, tragedy invades our lives.
Thus it was for Job.

There was a man named Job, living in the land of Uz,
who worshiped God and was faithful to him. He was

23

a good man, careful not to do anything evil. He had seven sons and three daughters . . . and was the richest man in the East. Job's sons used to take turns giving a feast, to which all the others would come, and they always invited their three sisters to join them. The morning after each feast, Job would get up early and offer sacrifices for each of his children in order to purify them. He always did this because he thought that one of them might have sinned by insulting God unintentionally (1:1-5).

With a few deft strokes the writer of the Book of Job tells us what this man Job was like.

An agriculturist, Job possessed herds so numerous that they "broke out in all directions," as the Hebrew words suggest. His wealth had increased until he was "the richest man in the East." Not only did he have enough to care amply for his family, but he had resources to alleviate human need. The poor, the widows, the orphans—all had found a benefactor in generous, righteous Job.

Yes, righteous. Although spectacularly successful in business, he had not lowered his morals or stooped to shady practices. He was "careful not to do anything evil," we read. He had placed faithfulness to God on the top of his value scale.

Job sought this faithfulness for his family as well. He had seven sons and three daughters. Seven, three, and ten are often biblical symbols of completeness, an indication of God's favor resting on Job.

Absorbed though he was in his work, Job loved his family; and the attention he gave them paid off. They were a close-knit family. They celebrated together. As is still the custom in some Eastern countries, each young adult son or daughter occupied a separate home, with all the homes built on the same big family compound. From time to time, one of Job's sons would give a party and invite the other brothers and sisters. It is worth noting that the sisters were included, for in those days women usually were held in low esteem. But not in Job's family.

Job was intensely earnest about his children's continuing to walk with God. Although they had not given him any trouble or caused him heartache, he did not rule out that possibility. Regularly, he assumed the role of mediator, going before God to plead His mercy and forgiveness on behalf of his children.

"In case they have unintentionally sinned, forgive them," he pleaded. And he "always" did this, we read. His concern was consistent and constant.

Job was no rookie in resisting temptation, either. According to his own statements, he had not lived for self. Nor could we accuse a successful man like him of laziness. No mention is made of his yielding to sexual temptation. Most remarkable of all, Job had been able to handle wealth and success and still remain true to God. Wealth brings power, and to hold power in your hand and still walk humbly with your God is no easy task.

Carlyle believed that for every hundred who can survive suffering, only one can handle sensational success. Job rates in the top one percent. Silver, success, selfishness, sloth, and sex have tripped up many people, causing them to fall into the arms of the evil one. Job had remained faithful to God in spite of his wealth.

Maybe, Satan thought, there is still a way to get him to turn his back on God. And so Satan set the trap of suffering and stepped back to watch.

Sooner or later suffering, in one form or another, visits us all. Being a child of God does not guarantee us continuing good health and success. It didn't for Job. It won't for us either. At one time or other in our lives, all of us will be tempted and tested.

How will we emerge? Trusting God, or cynical? How did Job emerge? Bitter, or better? Let us follow him through the valley and see what happens.

We have to pitch our tents where we shall always have quiet times with God, however noisy our times with the world may be.

—Oswald Chambers

You Can't Grow Faith Overnight

> The morning after each feast, Job would get up early and offer sacrifices for each of his children in order to purify them. He always did this because he thought that one of them might have sinned by insulting God unintentionally. . . . [God said,] "He worships me and is careful not to do anything evil" (1:5,8).

We were walking through the redwood forests in northern California when we came upon a giant tree that had fallen victim to man's steel saw, lying now on its side on the mossy, leaf-covered forest floor. A plaque by the side of the tree called attention to the tree's great age and pointed out the differing widths of the tree's growth rings. The plaque also explained that the tree grew most rapidly when it was not choked out or overshadowed by other trees, when the warm rays of the sun could reach it. Favorable conditions of sufficient moisture and light and an absence of freezing cold or persistent strong winds produced the most rapid growth.

So too, days of sunshine, years when all goes well afford us the most favorable opportunities to grow in our faith, if we only have sense enough to realize this. True, times of grief and bereavement and trouble can drive us to God and the study of His Word. But it is also during these times that we often are so distracted by the trauma of our pain and loss that it is difficult to concentrate on, remember, or even grasp what we are being told.

Dr. Kübler-Ross, author of *On Death and Dying*, has noted that religious faith unquestionably sustains people during times of grief; but faith cannot be developed over-night. This is one of the reasons sudden deaths cause such overwhelming trauma, for people are caught unprepared.

So rather than being a time of rapid growth, times of stress and testing may simply reveal the character that has been developed in us during the good days. Our walk with God is much more of a tortoise walk than the hop-skip-jump of the rabbit with naps in between. If, during our good days, we practice making the appropriate responses to God, those responses eventually will seem natural to us when testing comes.

We need to note, however, one difference between trees and us and growth is that the trees' growth appears to be a natural, spontaneous outcome. For us, spiritual growth during sunny days of blessing will come only as a result of steadfast, patient discipline. We set aside time every day for orderly reading of the Word, for praise, prayer, reflection, and meditation. We enrich our lives further by disciplined study of the Word and by inquiring into the in-sights of others. And, most important of all, we act on what we know, for, as Oswald Chambers noted, it sometimes is possible to grow more through five minutes of obedience than five years of study.

The trouble is that while a disciplined life of this nature at first challenges us and then begins to yield some benefits, as the days pass the discipline assumes more of a restrictive role, and results are not as immediate or apparent. Then the temptation to ease the discipline and sink back into old

habit patterns grows stronger and stronger. We find ourselves face to face with a stubborn resistance which we must
overcome. For we must doggedly persevere until finally the
new habit of discipline becomes such an integral, pleasant
part of our lives that we would miss it if it were absent. And
it is the fruit of that sustained discipline that surely will be
evident in the days of testing.

E. Stanley Jones relates in his last book, *The Divine
Yes*, that it was during his years at an evangelical college
that he established the habit of spending approximately two
hours a day in Bible study and prayer, prayer that included
quiet times to listen and meditate. He underlined and filled
the margins of his Bible with notes as he studied. At the
end of the day he entered in a journal things he had read
during the day he wanted to note, as well as significant
personal experiences of the day.

Jones' life embraced 50 years of missionary service in
India, in addition to a worldwide evangelistic ministry. He
also authored 28 books, two of which became best sellers.

He had looked forward "to a gentle descent into his
nineties." Then at age 87, following a series of evangelistic
meetings in Japan, while he was continuing with meetings
in Oklahoma City, seeming tragedy struck. The following
morning he was to conduct healing services. During the
night he awakened to go to the bathroom. On the way back
to bed, his left leg collapsed under him. He fell to the floor,
his entire left side now paralyzed. Unable to call out for help,
he lay on the floor for several hours. Finally he was able to
inch himself back to bed, but lay there helpless. At seven
in the morning someone came to ask why he had not come
to the healing meetings that had been announced. He could
not answer. The door was locked from the inside. Finally
friends gained entrance through a window and hurried him
off to a hospital. The only part of his body not affected were
the brain passages that preside over the intelligence. "The
glorious thing was that my faith was not shattered," Jones

wrote later. "I was not holding it; it was holding me. I can honestly say I wasn't asking, 'My God, why?' I could, and I can face the future with him."

A year later in a rehabilitation hospital he acknowledged that his eyesight still was cut in half, and his speech barely intelligible. He was practically immobile. He had been trying to learn to walk again like a baby, but not experiencing much success. "But am I unhappy?" he asked. "If so, I haven't discovered it. I belong to an unchanging Person. Jesus is the Divine Yes when there isn't much yes in my surroundings to rejoice in, except in him."

He went on to describe how in Switzerland the Swiss climbers have a rope, the strands of which are strongest at the center. So strong are they that those strands can hold up a person even when all the outer edges have been frayed away. Jones said he had found the same to be true for him. He noted that many of the strands of his life had been broken by the stroke. He could no longer write nor preach. He tried to express himself by dictating into a tape recorder. "The things that were dear to me, for the time being, are broken," he said. "The innermost strands belonging to Jesus and my experiences of him hold me as much as the total rope. I need no outer props to hold up my faith, for my faith holds me."

Not many of us are able to spend two hours every day in Bible study and prayer. Nor has it been given to us to have the illustrious career that E. Stanley Jones enjoyed. Most of us are just ordinary people for whom the affairs of living consume a majority of our time. But if we are faithful in using some time every day in staying in touch with our God, we shall find that for us too, when the outer strands of our ropes break, the inner strands will support us.

Job, as we shall discover, did experience anger. But Job also lived the other side of Christ's resurrection and the new insight it brings to life for us. And although Job did

30

struggle and had questions and was angry with God, still he never doubted God's existence.

Whatever our experiences may be, the days, weeks, months and years that each of us practices trusting God will stand us in good stead when difficult days come. We *will* be stronger.

Consider it pure joy, my brothers, whenever you
face trials of many kinds, because you know that
the testing of your faith develops perseverance. . . .
When tempted, no one should say, "God is
tempting me." For God cannot be tempted by
evil, nor does he tempt anyone; but each one is
tempted when, by his own evil desire, he is
dragged away and enticed.

—James 1:2, 3, 13, 14, NIV

Two Aspects of Suffering

When the day came for the heavenly beings to
appear before the Lord, Satan was there among
them. The Lord asked him, "What have you been
doing?" Satan answered, "I have been walking
here and there, roaming the earth." The Lord
said, "Did you notice my servant Job?" (1:6-8).

The writer of the Book of Job pulls aside the curtain and
lets us in on the "other-worldly" reasons for the troubles
that are about to descend on Job. Job and his friends are
not told of this. Only we, the readers and observers of the
drama, know.

So there is a heavenly reason for the earthly conflict.
Both God and Satan are interested in what happens to Job.
James referred to this dual conflict in his epistle when he
stated that God tries and tests us through the difficult experiences of our lives, while Satan tempts us. The dual nature of the tension we experience probably could be

compared with the conflicting forces we feel when we walk up the steps of a pool. The water both buoys us up and pulls us down.

Frequently, however, we are so absorbed in how to cope with the tragedies and troubles that hit us that we don't think of God's or (perhaps even more so) Satan's interest in what is happening to us. "The devil's boots don't creak," a Scottish proverb declares. Satan prefers that we do not think of him; he operates with a low profile. Awareness of both God's and Satan's interest in our troubles should strengthen our resolve to respond positively to God.

Doctrine without experience is truth without confirmation.

—Oscar Blackwelder

We prefer the spurious rest of spiritual coma to the restlessness of true discipleship.

—Gerhard E. Frost

But, God, It Hurts When You Stretch Me!

"Did you notice my servant Job?" the Lord asked (1:8).

If God really loved Job, why did He call Satan's attention to him and even suggest Satan might like to try to tempt him? Don't we pray, "Lead us not into temptation"? A difficult question, indeed.

And if Job was as upright and righteous as the opening sentences declare him, why didn't God leave things as they were? Yet another difficult question. To answer these questions is to presume to know the mind of God.

But against the backdrop of what we know about the thoughts and intents of God from other portions of Scripture, perhaps we can venture a guess.

Why do we exist at all? To glorify God, some say. To have fellowship with God, to satisfy God's own heartfelt longings for companionship, others say.

34

To have any relationship with God at all calls for faith, because God is unseen. By faith we believe God exists. By faith we believe Christ died for our sins and thereby made possible for us a comfortable relationship with God. By faith we believe in the Resurrection and an eternal life and a relationship with God after death.

None of these things can be scientifically proven. We believe that they are true. We live and walk and die by faith. Jesus repeatedly emphasized that participation in the on-going life with God will come only as we have faith. Thus our chief earthly goal becomes the increase of our faith. So important is faith that psychologist Erich Fromm says that "without faith man becomes sterile, hopeless, and afraid to the very core of his being."

True faith is alive, and anything living is not static. It must either grow or die. And faith, painfully enough, is a plant that seems to require periodic fertilizing and pruning by testing and tension in order for it to remain healthy and sturdy.

The great faith chapter, Hebrews 11, traces the development of Abraham's faith through one testing after another. It began when Abraham was called to leave home, not knowing where he was to settle.

On one of our return trips from Africa we visted Sweden, the fatherland both of my husband's parents and mine. The aging minister in the parish where Luverne's grandfather had grown up showed us the ruins of the old homestead. He led us through a pasture to a little clump of whispering birch and pine trees; there, hidden in the tall grass, were the tumbled-down remains of the house. Only the vegetable cellar, dug into the stony ground, remained intact.

As we stood there, I pictured the young Swedish couple with their small children. During the long, gray, chilling months of winter, they talked at length as to whether they should venture to the New World. What tugs and pulls there

35

must have been! What a mixture of hope and fear. What would life be like in the new land? But how could they know without going? So one spring day they walked out of their little home and, with a few trunks and bundles, headed for Stockholm, the open sea, and finally America. What a venture of faith it was!

So it was with Abraham. He did not find a permanent place to settle right away. He was still in tents, but probably getting used to the life of a sojourner, when God called him to stretch his faith again.

Many years earlier God had made Abraham a threefold promise: (1) a new land; (2) a son, so that his progenitors eventually would number in the thousands, and (3) through them blessing which would touch all nations. God had asked Abraham to believe this at a time when there was no indication that any of it would ever come true.

But because of this promise Abraham dared to set out in search of a new land. Now it was time for God to ask Abraham to believe specifically that he would have a son. How ridiculous, Abraham could have thought. Why hadn't God acted earlier? He had delayed so long that it was humanly impossible now. Both he and Sarah were too old for childbearing.

"Oh, no, you aren't, if you will only believe Me!" God said. "I don't lie."

The years of previous testing had prepared Abraham. We read that at last Abraham was able to look all the facts in the face and believe that if God had said they would have a baby, they would have a baby.

So Isaac was born—a miracle baby.

God let Abraham relax and enjoy his son for a few years. Then suddenly, unexpectedly, God decided it was time for Abraham's faith to grow some more. So He ordered Abraham to sacrifice Isaac. Abraham struggled with this new call to obedience, so radical and unreasonable it was startling. But at last his faith reached out, and Abraham declared

36

that he believed even if Isaac died, God could raise him from the dead!

And so it continued for Abraham throughout life, until at last he was called to die in faith, not having seen all of God's promises to him completely fulfilled, but believing that in time they would be.

Abraham was a giant of faith. But he was not born thus. He became a person of faith through testing and through responding to challenge after challenge that God laid before him.

So it was for Job. He had stood by others in their crises and assured them God would see them through. He had comforted widows and had served as a father to orphans. Eliphaz reminded him of all this later. But how would he stand up when death robbed him of his loved ones? Would the words he had uttered so easily before be words he could say when he himself suffered? The trial of suffering would offer him yet another opportunity to discover for himself how authentic his declarations of faith really were.

So too, God gives us opportunities to discover how real our faith is. But who of us wants to be stretched in this way? We want a strong faith, but we shrink from the growing process. We'd rather be left alone and allowed to go our own comfortable way—our needs amply supplied, our loving family surrounding us, our snug life at church affirming us, our sensitivity to right and wrong a bit blunt, and our conscience not deeply disturbed.

We may be satisfied with our status quo, but God is not. He forever encourages us to explore further both our depths and His. And we can explore our depths only as we understand how much of our faith is real and how much is only imagined. And how do we know which is which until our faith is tested?

God knows. Our testings are not for His benefit, but for ours, that we may understand aright just where we truly stand, and realizing afresh our complete and utter help-lessness, turn to Him.

Sometimes in this process He releases His restraining power and lets evil attack. He allowed it for His Son. He will allow it for us too. Understanding this can help us greet trials and testings with trembling joy. Faith must be tested to prove how real it is. Better to be tested now than at the time of our own death.

Scene II
The Royal Court of Heaven

God, chief character: confident and assured, calm and in control.

Satan, opposing character: jealous, suave, restless, cynical, and challenging.

Other heavenly beings.

Reference: 1:6-12.

We have become so commercialized that we only go to God for something from Him, and not for Himself.

—Oswald Chambers

What's in It for Me?

Satan replied, "Would Job worship you if he got nothing out of it?" (1:9).

How well Satan knows us! Far more often than I like to admit, the question "What's in this for me?" lies hidden in my mind, leaping to consciousness when confronted with new situations, opportunities, or calls to duty.

What is there for me in this new friendship? What will I gain from joining this church or serving on this committee? How will my business, social, or intellectual life be benefitted by this association? All too quickly and frequently I evaluate opportunities and people in these terms. I don't like this aspect of me; in fact, I lament and despise it. But if I am to be honest, I must confess it is there.

This is partly so because I am an ambitious, goal-oriented person. Then my natural sinful bent cooperates willingly by encouraging me to put myself in the center of the picture. Our American culture further fortifies my "old Adam" by repeatedly telling me that as an individual I have certain inalienable rights, and that one of these rights is to be successful.

But sometimes this attitude is reflected in our communal church life also. We publicly and with ceremony welcome those who join our congregations. But when people move away, do we acknowledge their departure, thanking them for their service and wishing them Godspeed? We gain when they join; we lose when they leave. And all too often our attitude says we are interested in them only when we gain.

If this awful, selfish, grasping attitude has penetrated our human relationships, how can we be sure it has not tarnished our relationship with God?

"God, if I worship you, what will you give me? Forgiveness of my sins? Eternal life? Earthly success? Health? Friends? Love? Will you spare me from failure and suffering, from heartbreak and disappointment? Will you heal me? Will you help my business succeed?"

Does this reflect our attitude?

Droning across a desert highway one day, I flicked on the radio to break the monotony of the long, hot ride. To my amazement, during the next 90 minutes I heard three different preachers promise healing of every physical ill, the solving of every relational problem, and the guarantee of financial success.

One offered to mail handkerchiefs charged with power to heal even cancer. Another had his announcer voice the invitation to call him long distance and share any problems. He had just returned from the Holy Land, charged with power to solve hitherto unsolvable problems (for a small fee, of course). The third offered the "blessing of the wallet," especially to those who would make a contribution of $12 to his radio broadcast (he considered 12 a holy number— 12 tribes, 12 apostles . . .).

Even though we may not be deceived by such bizarre offers and requests, Satan's question remains a soul-searching one for all of us. How pure is my love for God? From what motive, really, do I serve Him? If I gained nothing, nothing at all, would I still love Him?

41

Ernest Gordon, Dean of the Chapel at Princeton University, in *Through the Valley of the Kwai* recounts his four years as a prisoner of war under the Japanese in Thailand and Burma. During his first year in Changi, on the east side of Singapore Island, 40,000 prisoners lived in an area meant to accommodate 1,000. Disease ran through the camp. Depression settled over the captives, and they began to give up hope. In their despair, Gordon writes, many turned to religion. Why?

"For most," Gordon declares, "religion was an attempt to find a quick and easy answer, a release from their fears. They believed that if they cajoled God properly He could be persuaded to rescue them from the miseries of their present existence. They prayed for food, for freedom, or to be spared from death. . . . One group assured me with absolute certainty that they knew the end of the war was at hand. When I asked them for proof, they told me they had found it in the books of Daniel and Revelation. They proceeded to demonstrate mathematically how they arrived at this conclusion."

Then Gordon goes on to observe: "The dominant motivation for such wholesale embracing of religion was not love and faith, but fear: fear of the unknown, fear of suffering, fear of the terror by night, fear of death itself, fear that made for division rather than community."

When the war did not come to an end quickly, when the men did not receive more food or were not spared from disease—in other words, when they could not manipulate God through their prayers—almost all of them turned their backs on Him and began to decline, until at last they were behaving in a fashion lower than animals.

As the Swedish theologian Ragnar Bring has noted: "True faith never makes God the servant." True faith will never follow God because of what we can get Him to do for us in answer to our prayers. True faith is found not in fear, but in love—the love of God first of all, which we see reflected in the life and death of Jesus. And then it is found in the love that is not self-centered, but other-directed, that asks not, "How much can I get out of this?" but rather, "How much can I give?"

When Thou callest me to go through the dark valley, let me not persuade myself that I know a way around.

—John Baillie

When Life Gives Us a New Assignment

"All right," the Lord said to Satan, "everything he has is in your power, but you must not hurt Job himself" (1:12).

Helen had thought she still had many years of an active, happy life ahead of her. Although she had been an efficient nurse, a mother who shared the interests and activities of her children, a homemaker who found satisfaction in creating a cozy, warm home atmosphere, it seemed now as if the future held only inactivity for her.

She gave away her nurse's uniforms. She tried to content herself with listening to her children tell what they had done. She fought frustration and discontent as she summoned strength to push TV dinners into the oven on her weakest days. Helplessly, she watched dust gather in her home.

Multiple sclerosis had claimed her as a victim.

"The hardest thing," she confessed one day, struggling for composure, "is being willing to be weak, to accept inactivity. I feel so worthless."

44

How difficult it is for us when life assigns us the task of suffering! This was quite a different assignment for Job, a prosperous man whose life to date had been caught up with business affairs and management! No longer would his productivity determine his value.

If we dare to generalize, we may say that suffering is even a more formidable assignment for a man than for a woman. American men have been conditioned to think they must succeed, succeed, succeed. To fail is embarrassing, so much so that many a male "failure," lacking the inner resources to survive personal tragedy and disaster, puts a pistol to his head or breathes from the exhaust pipe of his running car or leaps from his hotel window to the pavement below. For many people, life's meaning is measured in terms of the success they can achieve—success as the world defines it.

But when God is able to get us apart in a quiet place where we can think about the meaning of life in light of eternity's values, an inner revolution takes place. We begin to ask God what His plan for us is, telling Him we are ready to accept it whether it be important or unimportant in the eyes of the world. Then the testing comes. For often—perhaps always—God's call to us involves suffering in some form. We can either try to sidestep this type of suffering or seek to find our way through.

A friend, a pastor at the height of his prospering career, was stricken with a lingering, terminal disease. He laid aside his plans for church expansion and accepted his new assignment: showing his people how to die. He did this with realism, courage, faith, and dignity.

Another friend feels called to God to provoke a response from Christians to the needs of the hungry millions. It is an unpopular calling, especially when it touches people's life-styles and calls for change. It makes people squirm. "I refuse to let you make me feel guilty," many say. When my friend was pastor of a parish, some members even left. Giving to the church declined. Cutting remarks were made.

"I've pleaded with God to free me from this call," my friend told me one day, "but I cannot escape it. So I have resolved to accept it, and I'm trusting God to lead me to a position where I can make a significant contribution towards meeting the needs of the hungry."

How many of us, I wonder, are prepared to accept the assignment to help alleviate the suffering and to correct the injustices in our world today?

Some time ago I visited with one of the top consulting geologists of the United States. He is convinced that the energy problems and the threat of overpopulation, famine, and brooding resentment among the "have-nots" will not "go away." He expects (and he bases his expectations on fact and research) that conditions will only worsen. But his chief concern is this: When America is called on to suffer, will we have the moral fiber and stamina to endure? Will we who have been raised to succeed and to prosper and to put ourselves in the center of the picture be able to accept voluntarily a new assignment, to adopt a simpler way of life and a lower standard of living?

How that can be worked out will vary, since each of us has different values and needs. But for all, it surely can mean being less wasteful, eating less meat, spending less for recreation and entertainment, putting on more clothes in the winter and perspiring a little in the summer, buying clothes of such a style that we can wear them longer, being more careful in our use of water, light, plastic, and paper goods—there is much all of us can do, and without pain or suffering either! But will we?

Bishop Hans Lilje of Germany, commenting on the factors that led to the downfall of the Third Reich, noted that "the individual citizen in the Third Reich had lost his power to play at this critical moment in history *because he had fallen prey to materialism and selfishness, to such an*

46

extent that he was no longer capable of making any sacrifice" (italics mine).

If the next assignment God gives you involves suffering in some form, will you be able to accept it? Will it help if you remember that the hands that hold out the assignment to you are the calloused, work-hardened hands of a carpenter who was born into a poor home, hands that are scarred because He allowed nails to pierce them for your sake?

Job is about to be given an assignment of suffering. Let us see in what form it comes to him.

Scene III
Job's Home

Job, chief character: devout, restrained in his grief.

The four messengers.

Reference: 1:13-22.

One trouble calls another on and gathers
overhead, Falls splashing down, till round my soul
a rising sea is spread.

—Nahum Tate

Shock and Praise

It happened the day Job's eldest son invited his brothers
and sisters to a feast at his house. Let's read the account.

> A messenger came running to Job. "We were plowing
> the fields with the oxen," he said, "and the donkeys
> were in a nearby pasture. Suddenly the Sabeans at-
> tacked and stole them all. They killed every one of
> your servants except me. I am the only one who es-
> caped to tell you."
>
> Before he had finished speaking, another servant
> came and said, "Lightning struck the sheep and the
> shepherds and killed them all. I am the only one who
> escaped to tell you."
>
> Before he had finished speaking, another servant
> came and said, "Three bands of Chaldean raiders at-
> tacked us, took away the camels, and killed all your
> servants except me. I am the only one who escaped
> to tell you."
>
> Before he had finished speaking, another servant
> came and said, "Your children were having a feast at
> the home of your oldest son, when a storm swept in
> from the desert. It blew the house down and killed them
> all. I am the only one who escaped to tell you" (1:14-
> 19).

50

Unbelievable tragedy and sorrow descended on Job with the suddenness of a tornado or a devastating earthquake.

We live in an earthquake-prone area. When the earthquake of 1970 struck, the Los Angeles area had been quiet, and life had been going on normally. Then, suddenly, there was heaving and shaking and mighty rumblings. Concrete roads snapped in two. Freeway overpasses came crashing down. Buildings swayed and crumpled. Inside houses, cupboard doors swung open, and dishes and groceries came crashing out. Pianos slid across rooms. And then all was quiet again—too quiet, for all around lay death and destruction.

So too it happened for Job. One hour all was normal. The next, nothing remained the same.

What was Job's first reaction? Numb, not really taking in what had happened, Job mouthed the appropriate response he had learned in Sunday school.

"The Lord gave, and now he has taken away. May his name be praised," he says in verse 21.

Many of us mistakenly have thought that those words reflect Job's only response to his suffering, and we have been agitated by those words. He uttered them too easily, we think. The words give no evidence that Job struggled to a position of resignation and acceptance.

When we bump into disappointments or sorrow or loss, it just isn't that easy. We know we should accept whatever is sent us and even offer God praise for what He will do through it, but we are often unwilling and unable to do so. Oh, because of the expectations of Christian friends we might say the right words and summon bright smiles. But inside we are bleeding.

I was. After the death of our two little sons I smiled and assured people God must have a purpose in it. I knew this was the expected response. But all the while anger, disappointment, doubt, rebellion, and confusion were churning

51

in my heart. My faith in God was badly shaken, and I was dismayed that as God's child I should be experiencing doubt and depression and anger. Have you ever felt this way?

What a relief and comfort then, for those of us who struggle, to read further and discover that Job also rode the dizzying roller coaster of unpredictable, varying emotions, and he too questioned God's love and justice. We realize then, that Job was probably in a state of shock when he uttered those magnificent words, "The Lord gave, and now he has taken away. May his name be praised." He had not yet fully comprehended the sweep and finality of his loss, that his life would never be the same again.

Occasionally, at a funeral or during the days immediately following the death of a husband, we see an almost ecstatic widow. Tearless, her face glows radiantly. She talks confidently of her joy that her loved one has gone to be with the Lord. She testifies to God's sustaining grace. We marvel at her strong, triumphant faith. But in reality, she may not have comprehended yet the finality or immensity of her loss, nor the pain she is going to experience as she learns to transfer her love for the one now dead to someone or something else. Mercifully, God often allows this ecstatic interlude in order for bereaved ones to prepare themselves for the long, difficult days ahead.

Not that Job's declaration was not the right one to make. It was "The Lord gave, and now he has taken away." It is right that we acknowledge His sovereignty. "May his name be praised."

But if in the midst of overwhelming, bewildering, and especially sudden sorrow you find yourself unable to praise the Lord sincerely from your heart, do not despair nor feel guilty. C. S. Lewis spoke of "the separation that agonizes." Genuine acceptance does not come easily, and never painlessly. Not even for righteous Job.

My harvest withers. Health, my means to live—
All things seem rushing straight into the dark.
But the dark still is God.

—George MacDonald

I haven't the right to choose the wood of my
cross.

—Michel Quoist

Oh, My Poor Body!

Then Satan left the Lord's presence and made
sores break out all over Job's body (2:7).

You overpower a man . . . . He feels only the pain
of his own body and the grief of his own mind
(14:20, 22).

The day Conrad Lund, president of the Seattle Lutheran
Bible Institute, was to submit to brain surgery, a friend of
his, Phil Butler, carried to the hospital this message from
the writings of George MacDonald:

We cannot yet have learned all that we are meant to
learn through the body. It is through the body that we
are both trained outwards from ourselves and driven
inwards into our deepest selves to find God. How much
of the teaching even of this world can the most diligent
and most favored men have exhausted before he is
called to leave it.

In commenting on the physical pain his wife, Joy, suffered as she lay dying of cancer, C. S. Lewis noted in his book *A Grief Observed*:

> Whatever fools may say, the body can suffer twenty times more than the mind. The mind has always some power of evasion. At worst, the unbearable thought only comes back intermittently, but the physical pain can be absolutely continuous. . . . Grief is like a bomber circling around and dropping its bombs each time the circle brings it overhead; physical pain is like the steady barrage on a trench in World War One, hours of it, with no let-up for a moment.

Poor Job! He, like Joy Davidson Lewis, lived before the day of Brompton's Mixture, the medication that today brings so much relief to dying people in pain. Added to his grief is the steady, gnawing, unrelenting pain of a body no longer at ease with itself.

An added tragedy for Job is that no one appears to do anything to relieve the pain. We see no one cleansing his sores, pouring ointment on them, bathing his body, or lovingly placing him to rest between cool, clean sheets on a comfortable bed. No one puts ice to his parched lips or a cool cloth to his fevered brow. No one lowers the light and sits by his side either to silently hold his hand or offer the comfort of distraction by playing soft music or flashing peaceful nature scenes on the wall at the foot of the bed. For us in this land with magnificently-equipped hospitals, staffed by skilful, able medical workers of every discipline, complete with pharmacies lined with shelves loaded with medications of every kind, and with health insurance a part of almost every work contract, Job's situation seems incredible, unbelievable. But not so for millions, yes, *millions* in third world countries.

My first encounter with physical suffering that should not have been necessary came while I was studying the

Nepali language in the Himalayas of northern India. Visiting a home, I found a young mother clasping her two-year-old son to her breast, rocking back and forth on her heels, wailing. The child she held was dead. So infested had he become with intestinal parasites that the worms had come crawling up his throat, choking him to death.

Unnecessary death in this age of enlightenment in which we live? Yes, and it happened simply because enough people did not care enough so this mother could get the basic hygienic teaching she needed.

That incident was but the beginning of my encounters with what seemed senseless suffering. In the years that followed, both in India and Africa, I witnessed case after case of physical suffering, unalleviated chiefly because there were not enough who cared. So Job's story, though written so many centuries ago, continues to reflect the misery of people who suffer physically with no one by their side to relieve the suffering.

Job's friends have not shown up yet although they will appear soon on the scene. But when they come, they first attempt to silently comfort, then to talk and then to preach. But not one does a thing to ease Job's physical suffering. "What next, Lord, what next?" we can hear Job crying. "Why, why does the body have to suffer?" Added to the pain of body for Job is the pain of a mind tortured with questions.

C. S. Lewis agonized over this question both before and after his wife's death. Finally he concluded, in essence, that it must be necessary. Why it is necessary remains a mystery. But if it is not necessary, he wrote, a good God would not permit it.

A dear friend of mine, Paul Lindell, himself smitten with cancer which eventually drained life from him, referred to pain as a mystery. In his little book *The Mystery of Pain* he noted that while God never sends pain, he does allow it. He referred to Luke 22:31-32; 1 John 5:19 and Acts 12:1-

2 as examples. Yet he acknowledged that "the power and willingness of Jesus to deliver from pain is surely unlimited. And he has promised this power to be used by his followers too. But only now and then do we see someone who is able to throw off pain and go home well and whole. Some stand up and shed their pains like old garments while others are wrapped up in the same pains as in a shroud and are carried off to their graves. No amount of medicine, surgery, prayer, anointing with oil, laying on of hands, or fasting and prayer has been able to bring healing to some of those we would most like to see healed. Why is this? Why is the gap between God's healing power and deliverance so wide and unbridgeable? And so the mystery stubbornly remains."

However, Paul said when he learned to see pain in perspective, he began to grow in understanding.

> "I understand that when I am reasonably well and free of illness, I know that I am enjoying the good provision of God in the first and the old creation of which I am still very much a part . . . At the same time I know that this is only temporary.
>
> "I understand that when I get sick, my pains are telling me that I am mortal . . . I accept this and make ready to lay down my body and surrender it to the earth any time, as it may please God. While I walk on this earth, I walk in the body that was made for this creation. When at last I walk on the new earth I will have a new body that will be given to me by God for that new realm.
>
> "I understand that when the Spirit gives me foretastes of the new creation, whether by his witness of sonship, his gifts for service, his healing for my bodily pains, or his strength for life's duties, then I sing Hallelujah, for I know and believe that we shall soon be changed. 'For this perishable nature must put on the imperishable, and this mortal nature must put on im-

56

mortality . . . Then shall come to pass the saying that
is written: Death is swallowed up in victory.' "

For us who live this side of Christ's resurrection and
who know we do not need to take the account of the resurrection with a pinch of salt, we can gain some insight into
the mystery of pain. Job, however, does not know about
Christ's resurrection. All he knows is that he hurts, in every
way, and no relief seems forthcoming.

Scene V
The Garbage Dump

Job: miserable, covered with sores, despondent.

Job's wife: irritated and worried.

Reference: 2:7-10.

> When the risk of being judged or betrayed arises,
> then the temptation comes to run away from it by
> keeping back certain confidences.
>
> —Paul Tournier

No Help from Our Loved Ones

> Job went and sat by the garbage dump and took
> a piece of broken pottery to scrape his sores (2:8).

I wonder what kind of relationship Mr. and Mrs. Job had. We do not read of Job turning to his wife for comfort. Instead, he runs away.

Of course, this might not be too strange, really. Psychologists tell us that in a very high percentage of the cases where a husband and wife are bereaved of a child, they experience marital problems within a year's time. And Mr. and Mrs. Job had suffered multiple bereavements and loss.

But still we wonder . . . that is, until we examine more closely the recorded conversation between them. We find Mrs. Job speaking first. Her impulsive outburst may give us an insight as to why Job had not sought her for comfort.

In the first place, Mrs. Job doesn't seem concerned about finding out how much Job is hurting. She tells him. And she tells him in an accusing, disapproving fashion. We can almost feel Job stiffening his back and pulling away from her.

And then she shoots out what seems to be cruel advice. "Curse God, and die" (2:9, RSV). It would appear that she is actually blaming Job for all their troubles because he trusted in God, at the same time suggesting that God brought it down on their heads!

Poor Job! He hasn't asked for advice. Paul Tournier observes: "Often men are just as easily hurt as women, even though they hide it. They are afraid of being hurt by advice just as much as by criticism. They resent it every bit as much."

Poor Mrs. Job! If only she had understood some of the verbal roadblocks that erect walls between people.

Ordering, commanding. "Curse God!"

Admonishing. "You should. You ought."

Interpreting. "You still trust God, don't you?"

Judging, which was inferred by her remarks.

Advising. "I'll tell you what to do."

One wonders if she used some of the other roadblocks to communication, too.

Logic. "What you need to understand is . . ."

Name-calling. "Stupid! Idiot! You look so dumb sitting here in the dump!"

Reassuring and sympathizing also can be a roadblock. "Don't worry; everything will work out."

Or, "When my father died, I didn't haul myself off to the village dump."

How much better if Mrs. Job would have sat down on the garbage beside her husband. Surely if she had sat there long enough, trying to enter into his hurt with him, forgetting her own sorrow—immensely difficult as that would be—and trying to understand how he was feeling, Job would have started to talk. And then, perhaps she could have had sense enough not to say much. "Uh-huh," maybe. Or she could have reached out for his hand, and when he was ready she could have moved a little closer. She could have felt her way along. And after a while she could have started

61

slowly, and just a bit at a time, to tell him how she was hurting.

And how much better it would have been if Job hadn't reacted by withdrawing. He gave her one quick retort.

"You speak as one of the foolish women would speak," he said (2:10, RSV).

Actually, in English it isn't as stinging a reply as it was in the original language. "Foolish" meant "one who lacks understanding of or belief in God." Remember the verse, "Fools say to themselves, 'There is no God' " (Ps. 14:1)? So it was as though Job were saying, "You speak as one who is not trusting God."

And this was true.

We must remember also that we cannot hear Job's tone of voice. It may be that instead of speaking sharply there was pathos and sorrow in his voice.

But either way, whether he scolded or gently reprimanded, he made no further attempt to communicate, but withdrew within himself.

How sad! Job desperately needed to be able to unload his feelings on someone who loved him and who would try to understand. How much better it would have been if he had said to himself, "I think I'm going to have a hard time getting her to understand how I really feel, but I'm going to keep on trying." How much better if he had risked further misunderstanding by venturing to talk. By not talking he put up a wall, and then he wondered later why he was so lonely. Those who complain that no one understands them need to ask themselves if one of the reasons is because they have not dared to bare their souls to others.

How sad for Mrs. Job too! Is there anything more frustrating for a wife than to know her husband is troubled and anxious about something but have him refuse to share it with her? I can almost hear Mrs. Job going back to her sisters and complaining, "If only he would talk, but he just sits there and scratches himself!"

There they were, both hurting desperately, both needing each other, both in a position where they could have helped each other so much—and neither knew how to reach out and communicate. And so the walls went up a little higher, and new hurts were added to old hurts, and loneliness set in.

To their credit, however, may it be noted that, although they misunderstood each other at the outset, they evidently became compatible later. How else can we account for the birth of 10 more children? The story does not tell us how Mr. and Mrs. Job learned to communicate, for this is not the central issue of the story. But we feel good in the knowledge that conflict and misunderstanding between husbands and wives during times of stress can be resolved happily in the end.

Walk in the forest when the storm is past and see how seldom a branch is broken except where it connects with the trunk or another branch. Character is most severely tested at the point of relationship. This is where storms tear and torture both trees and human beings.

—Gerhard E. Frost

Wounding Those We Love

His wife said to him, "You are still as faithful as ever, aren't you? Why don't you curse God and die?" (2:9).

Mrs. Job is hurting.

Gone is her security.

Gone is her husband's source of income. Brigands and robbers have either killed the herds or driven them away to another land.

Gone also is her husband's health. And what is more threatening to a wife than for her husband to become seriously ill? With the loss of health goes the loss of ability to work, and without a job there is no income.

Gone, also, in one swift blow, are all her children whom one by one she had carried in the warm, dark recesses of her body. Though a knife severed them from her when the umbilical cords were cut, still she can remember those months when she and her children were "one flesh." As a mother she has felt uniquely close to her children, so that now losing all 10 of them through death is one of the most grievous bereavements she will ever know. Ten parts of her have died.

Added to all this, her husband has become physically repulsive. His sores stink so that she cannot stand to get near him, just at the time when she longs to feel his strong protecting arm around her and bury her face in his chest.

Poor Mrs. Job! She is completely beside herself. Angry, feeling threatened, and worried about the future, she doesn't know how to handle the effect the multiple disasters have had on her. And then as she is struggling with all of this, her husband disappears.

Fearful and anxious lest Job in his depressed state do away with himself, she runs to search for him, quite likely first at the homes of their friends. He is not there. She drags herself home to find him at last, of all places, in back of the compound where the garbage is dumped. He is crouching there like an animal among the rubbish, scraping himself with pieces of broken pottery. She is relieved to find him, but angry because she thinks he isn't acting the part of a brave man, strong enough to give her the courage and hope she so desperately needs. In stinging anger she lashes out.

"You are still as faithful as ever, aren't you?" she taunts. "Why don't you curse God and die?"

Extraordinary advice! Has Mrs. Job really thought through what she is saying? Or is she venting the anger she feels because her husband seems to be coping so poorly? Is she feeling frustrated because she does not know how to help him cope? Does this intensify her own feeling of in-security to the point that she becomes so enraged with him that she actually wishes him dead? Insecurity often makes us very angry. When we do not know how to deal with a situation involving a loved one, we often lash out in anger.

I know a Christian father whose son is schizophrenic. The father has felt so helpless that in deep anger he as rejected his son. So, too, now for Mrs. Job. The two most dearly loved ones in her life, God and her husband, become the targets of her raging, uncomprehending, confused anger.

How sad that when we ourselves are hurting we often wound those we love the most!

A couple I know were having difficulty in their marriage relationship. The wife, the stronger-willed of the two, longed for her husband to become more assertive and assume more responsibility for disciplining the children. She felt she was carrying an unfair share of the parenthood load.

One evening the arguing started and quickly crescendoed into a rage. White-hot with anger, his wife poured forth an unbelievable stream of accusations and bitterness, calling her husband name after name. Then suddenly she saw him crumple. His face, twisted with emotion, told her that she had dealt a fatal blow to his self-esteem, and probably to their love. She fell on the couch weeping and sobbing. Then her husband—bless him!—walked over, sat down beside her, and gathered her tenderly in his arms. They sat together, both of them weeping.

"We knew," she confessed, "that such awful things had been said and such deep wounds had been inflicted that no human would ever be able to correct things again. So still weeping, we fell to our knees and pleaded with God. We asked each other's forgiveness. We asked God's forgiveness. We begged His cleansing power. We entreated His healing. After a long time, our sobs subsided, and finally we helped each other to our feet and stood locked in a tender, warm embrace. Deep peace engulfed us, and we knew God had wrought a miracle and had brought healing that would not have been possible otherwise."

From that point on, the couple set about consciously and earnestly to learn to communicate with each other—practicing daily. They tried to understand that each had certain needs to be met. Both of them learned to adapt and change. The result has been a strong and beautiful marriage, with each of them unusually sensitive to the other.

But to get back to Mrs. Job, instead of condemning her, should we not rather let her behavior and her words warn us? Do we wives sometimes wrong our husbands by expecting them always to be strong and in control of situations as well as of their emotions? Do we deny them the right to be human, to struggle, to feel weak, to make mistakes? Do we cut away at their self-esteem by sarcastically calling attention to poor performance? Do we become angry with them when they continue to assert faith in God when we feel God has let us down?

When anger, anxiety, or bitter bereavement mount to an unbearable pitch, instead of wounding with words, is it not better to vent our emotions by pedaling a bicyle or by jogging, by pounding a wall or by kneading bread?

This is not to deny the necessity to put into words how we feel. But we should choose wisely one who can listen objectively, unaffected by what we say, one who can wisely discern what is really meant.

When we explode verbally, we need to learn not to attack others. We need to say, "I am angry," stating our emotion, rather than, "You make me furious," thus blaming another for our reactions.

Likewise, as we struggle with our own private battles, we need to be aware of how our words affect the attitudes of our families or others who hear us. We need to ask God to keep us from sinning with our lips by uttering those unbelieving, accusing statements that may cause a weaker member of our family to slip into resentment and bitterness and unbelief. And it can be an act of faith on our part to say, even though we do not yet *feel* assured, "God will see us through."

> A man's foes will be those of his own household.
>
> —Matthew 10:36, RSV

When Those We Love Don't Understand

> His wife said to him, "You are still as faithful as ever, aren't you? Why don't you curse God and die?" (2:9).

If Satan can't get at us any other way, he will try to reach us through those we love the most: a spouse, children, parents, brothers and sisters, a close friend, a respected teacher. Perhaps it is never more difficult to recognize the evil one's presence than when he comes in this guise.

Jesus experienced temptation in this form too. As His ministry was becoming more and more publicized, talk about Him spread throughout the land. The talk kindled antagonistic feelings, and those feelings were fanned into strong passions. Still Jesus continued on course, not toning down His declarations nor ceasing to perform miracles. Even more serious, Jesus seemed determined to go to Jerusalem, where feeling against Him burned hottest and where radicals often incited mob action. This troubled His followers, who were concerned about His safety.

"He's crazy!" many declared, thinking that His bold declarations that He was divine revealed an unstable mind. Others thought His seeming foolhardiness in courting danger indicated an unsound mind.

Did these rumors reach the members of Jesus' family in Nazareth? Is this what prompted them to go in search of Him while He was away on His second preaching tour (Luke 8:19-21)? Did they fear for His safety? Did they perhaps even want Him to come home where they could keep an eye on Him and control Him? For His own protection, of course, they might have thought.

Whatever their motivation, Jesus evidently saw in their visit a temptation to turn aside from the way of the Cross. When they arrived at the place He was staying, He refused to see them. Even more painful for them, He indicated that their close human family ties meant nothing to Him if they were going to stand in the way of His obeying God.

When a messenger told Him His mother and brothers were outside and wanted to see Him, He said, "My mother and brothers are those who hear the word of God and obey it" (Luke 8:21).

This must have been a slap in the face for Jesus' mother and brothers, a stinging, seemingly unloving rebuke. Yet Jesus had no choice. He had to refuse even those who loved Him most if they blocked His obedience to God.

So too for Job. He cannot afford the luxury of wallowing in the self-pity his wife has offered him and thus turn against God. His resolve has not yet weakened. If God has let all these troubles come into his life, he will accept them.

"You are talking nonsense!" he retorts to his wife. "When God sends us something good, we welcome it. How can we complain when he sends us trouble?" (2:10).

Many a young person and many a husband or wife married to a non-Christian experience again and again Satan's attack through a loved one. How often the suggestions are heard: "You can serve God without becoming a minister." "You can worship God without going to church." "You can be a good person without being a Christian." "You don't have to become a fanatic." "You don't need to spend so much time studying the Bible."

69

A young nurse felt God calling her to serve in a Christian hospital overseas. So violent was the reaction of her parents that they threatened to disown her. But the girl persisted in following her convictions. For seven years her parents would not even acknowledge her letters or write to her. In the end, God led her to a widower with children, and she found a new family unit to love, protect, and comfort her. "My father and mother may abandon me, but the Lord will take care of me," the psalmist reassures us (Ps. 27:10).

A young man discovered that the girl he loved was pulling away from God. She was accusing him of being too religious. She refused to read the Bible and pray with him. He wasn't fun anymore, she complained. For four days, after he returned home from work in the evenings, the young man shut himself in his room and read his Bible and prayed.

"The issue focused clearly for me," he said. "It was as though God were asking me who it was going to be: Gail or Him. Gail had become the dearest person in the world to me. Satan couldn't have tempted me in a more vulnerable area. But then Christ revealed Himself to me in all His love, and I knew I could live without Gail, but not without the Lord Jesus."

Poor Job! He has entered into a covenant relationship with Mrs. Job and is committed to her for life. But just now it seems things would have been better for him if she too had been swept away by the cyclone that took the lives of his children. At least that would have silenced her.

But God has included Mrs. Job in future plans for Job's blessing. So Job must put up with her, difficult as it is. At the same time, he must close his ears to her suggestive talk, because he realizes that listening will weaken his determination to be true to God. Satan must be resisted—even when he comes to us through those we love.

Scene VI
The Garbage Dump

Job: miserable, angry, despondent.

Eliphaz, Bildad, and Zophar: Job's three friends.

This section includes three series of dialogues between Job and his three friends.

Reference: 2:11—27:23.

The suffering of one who dies alone, while his family, in the adjoining room, wait for his death, drinking coffee.

—Michel Quoist

Don't just do something; stand there!

—William A. Miller

A Friend's Quiet Comfort

Then they sat there on the ground with him [Job] for seven days and nights without saying a word, because they [his friends] saw how much he was suffering (2:13).

Todd, the 15-year-old son of a friend of mine, was slowly dying of cancer. The young lad was in and out of the hospital. When he was not hospitalized, he was treated as an outpatient, and he and his mother spent hours in waiting rooms.

One such day, after Todd had gone in for treatment, Vivian, his mother, was sitting in the waiting room. A comfortably rounded Jewish woman sitting next to her began to chat and at last inquired what had brought Vivian to the hospital. Vivian told her. The Jewish lady sucked in her breath. She uttered but one word emphatically, and then sat silent.

"The word she uttered was one I do not choose to use," Vivian said, "but the silence that followed reached out to me and brought much more comfort than a tirade of sympathetic words ever would have."

William A. Miller writes in *Why Do Christians Break Down?*:

> If we can move in the direction of learning the ministry of being, hopefully we can relax the compulsion of always having to do something. That is not to say that doing does not have its place; but it is to say that being generally has been neglected in relationships, because doing is really easier and less risky . . . the most productive atmosphere for healing should be the human relationship wherein authentic love can be felt in terms of acceptance, empathy, compassion, warmth, and genuineness.

Roger Ose wrote in the *Lutheran Standard* of his battle with cancer.

> Some of my most difficult times here in the hospital room are when doctors and nurses are in a hurry and can't take time for me. Why are the doctors in such a hurry? Why are visitors in such a hurry? I remember one man who sat alone in my room for two hours while I was in surgery. He took time from his busy schedule just to wait. I don't remember what he said, but I remember he was there.

Ernest Gordon, writing of his years as a prisoner of the Japanese in the 1940s, tells of receiving word one day in camp that an 18-year-old lad who had been in his company had been asking to see him. Gangrene had spread over his whole body. He was dying—and he told Gordon he was afraid.

"What could I say?" Gordon asks. "I knew he didn't have a chance. I looked at him lying there so lonely, so young, and said the only thing I could think of. 'We'll help you not be scared. We'll stay with you.'

"That seemed to ease his mind," Gordon notes. " 'Thank you, Sir,' he said, 'That's good to know.' And he gave me an engaging boyish grin."

Gordon contacted other caring men in the camp and told them about the lad. Soon visitor after visitor appeared at the boy's sleeping platform. He was seldom alone.

One night when Gordon came, he found the lad relaxed and cheerful.

"You've no idea what a help it is to have friends," he said. "I don't feel lonely anymore. And I'm not scared."

And then he broached again the subject of death, and Gordon was able to introduce the lad to the Lord Jesus, the Good Shepherd who promises to walk with all of us through the valley of the shadow of death.

A few days later the lad died at peace, declaring it was all right. He knew God his Father was very near to him, he said.

We wonder, however, whether this frightened lad could have laid hold on faith in his God if first there had not been some of God's children willing to just sit with him.

I think, too, of an incident that took place during the years I lived among the Nepalese in northern India. My colleague, Becky Grimsrud, a nurse and midwife, had been summoned to a home where a young Tibetan mother was having difficulty giving birth to her child.

We stooped to enter the thatched hut and paused for a moment to let our eyes adjust to the darkness before we could see the young mother on the wooden plank bed. She was so frightened!

As Becky began her preparations, I stepped to the bedside and began to talk to the young mother. I stroked her cheeks and brushed back her black hair, wet with perspiration. I held her hand and soon, little by little, I saw the fear leave her huge brown eyes. Her taut body relaxed. She sighed and smiled and gave my hand a squeeze.

74

"It's so good to have you here," she said. "Since you came to our village, our homes have become light."

Do you have a sorrowing or depressed friend? Follow this example of Job's friends. Arise and go to them. If words don't come, don't worry. Your presence, a nonjudgmental ear, and physical touch will comfort.

Better is open rebuke than hidden love.
—Proverbs 27:5, RSV

Iron sharpens iron, and one man sharpens
another.
—Proverbs 27:17, RSV

Straight Talk

Job, we must admit, was a gusty, gutsy guy. His friends were no pansies either. The four men gave it to each other straight, without blinking. If they staggered, they didn't let repartee stop them, but came back for more.

Much of the humor of the book (and in spite of its somber topic, a lot of humor surfaces) is found in the explosive, honest exchange that passes among these four men. Listen to some of their remarks.

Bildad: Are you finally through with your windy speech? (8:1,2).

Job: Yes, I've heard all that [you've said] before (9:1).

Zophar: Will no one answer all this nonsense?
Does talking so much put a man in the right?
Job, do you think we can't answer you?
That your mocking words will leave us speechless? (11:1-3).

Job: Yes, you are the voice of the people.
When you die, wisdom will die with you (12:1,2).

Job: Everything you say, I have heard before.

76

I understand it all; I know as much as you do (13:1,2).

Eliphaz: Empty words, Job! Empty words!
No wise man would talk the way you do (15:1-3).

Job. The comfort you give is only torment
Are you going to keep on talking forever?
Do you always have to have the last word? (16:1-3).

Bildad: Job, can't people like you ever be quiet?
If you stopped to listen, we could talk to you (18:1,2).

Job: Why do you keep tormenting me with words? (19:1,2).

Zophar: Job, you upset me (20:1).

Admittedly, there seems to be little listening and even less understanding. But at least Job has found friends in front of whom he can verbally pour out his misery.

Dr. Elisabeth Kübler-Ross, who has talked with many dying people, believes that in most cases the listener does not have to come up with answers. If we can only be there and care about our suffering friends, the sufferers very often will see the solution themselves as they verbalize their distress. It is as though speaking about their problems helps them to look at them objectively; often they see what to do or what attitudes to adopt.

We find Job turning to his friends for free, open, honest discussion, and undoubtedly it was not the worst of bad solutions for him.

Sometimes, hard-trying, it seems I cannot pray—
For doubt, and pain, and anger, and all strife,
Yet some poor half-fledged prayer-bird
    from the nest
May fall, flit, fly, perch—
    crouch in the bowery breast
Of the large, nation-healing tree of life;
Moveless there sit through all the burning day,
And on my heart at night a fresh leaf cooling lay.

—George MacDonald

I Want to Die!

Finally Job broke the silence and cursed the day
on which he had been born . . . . "I wish I had
died in my mother's womb or died the moment
I was born" (3:1, 11).

The death wish. Who is not acquainted with it in one form
or another?

"The day after our child died," a father shared, "I
looked out the window at the geraniums outside. Their
bright colors always used to cheer me. This morning they
seemed to have lost their color. They looked faded and
drab. My breakfast was tasteless. My work, which I had
always enjoyed previously, now held no appeal for me. I
didn't even seem to care for our children who still remained
alive. I hurt so much I wanted to die."

Even those of us who have not suffered the loss of
someone very dear to us know days when life goes gray

78

and the zest for living is gone. An adolescent, looking in the mirror morning after morning at a face scarred with acne, can become so depressed he wishes he could end it all. An overweight girl blames her parents for a genetic tendency to gain weight easily and angrily wishes she could be free from what they have passed on to her.

What shall we do when people tell us they wish to die? In most cases it's natural for all of us to feel this way from time to time. Telling people they shouldn't feel that way or that they should cheer up and remember all the things they have to live for doesn't help. Instead, that usually makes them feel resentful and rebellious, and they will turn away, saying to themselves, "Now I know they don't understand how I feel."

There are, of course, those exceptional cases when depression persists and worsens. Skilled help should then be sought for the suffering one. But Job's depression is not of this type. His is the darkness that frequently follows bereavement.

Be patient with those like Job. Allow them to say outrageous, shocking things. Love them. Hold them tenderly if they will let you. If they push you away or don't want you to touch them, don't. Get out of their way. Allow them the privacy they are asking for. Don't try to prevent their suffering, either. Out of suffering comes real healing. And as healing continues, the death wish will be voiced less and less often, and eventually it will fade away completely. Broken hearts can heal. Scars will remain, yes, but scars are but an emblem of an encounter with suffering—a badge of courage, someone has noted.

Listen, I'll let you in on a secret! The bugle will blow, and the dead will live again—eternally—and we shall be changed. For this decaying body has to be outfitted with immortality. When this outfitting takes place, then the Bible verse will come true when it says: "Death sure took a licking. Say, Death, what have you won? And Death, what happened to your stinger?" Sin is death's stinger, and sin's power is the law. Thank you, God, for giving us the victory through our Lord Jesus Christ.

— 1 Corinthians 15:51, 53-57, Cotton Patch Version

Need the Thought of Death Bring Gloom?

They [people] are not happy till they are dead and buried (3:22).

What is your attitude toward death?

Different people in different ages and with different religious beliefs view death in different ways.

Herodotus, the Greek historian, relates the custom of the Thracians. When a child was born, the family would weep in anticipation of all the trouble and sorrow he would have to face. When a person died, however, the family would laugh and sing and rejoice, for now that person was set free.

The early Christians, for the first three hundred years, celebrated only two festivals: Easter, which commemorated Christ's winning eternal life for us because of His resurrection; and a person's own death day. As they looked at it, a person's death day ushered him into a new life with God, and thus they could anticipate death with joy.

The Jews of Jesus' day thought of an ongoing life chiefly as a life lived on by one's children and grandchildren. For Job, whose children had all been killed by a tornado, no guarantee of a happy continuing life remained. All he could anticipate now was Sheol, the place of the dead. And who could draw comfort from Sheol? In one of Job's conversations he describes what he anticipates: "I am going soon and will never come back—going to a land that is dark and gloomy, a land of darkness, shadows, and confusion, where the light itself is darkness" (10:21, 22).

But even though he envisioned such a gloomy, uncertain future, Job longed for it because he thought anything would be better than his painful present.

What is your attitude toward death? Many of us fear it and try to deny it. Some superstitiously believe that if we talk or read about it, it might happen to us. Most of us, if we are honest, shrink from death. It represents a threat to our sense of security, for one thing. We know this present life is real, and even though it ladles out to us trouble and discomfort from time to time, things have to become very desperate before we want to cease living. After all, we ask ourselves in the deepest recesses of our mind, how can we be sure of a life beyond death? We have to admit that our only guarantee is that Jesus rose again, and that God's Word declares there is life for those who know Him. We accept that Word as truth.

We fear death also because we were created to live, not to die. Death is an intruder, an enemy.

But death is an enemy that was overcome by Christ's death and resurrection. It is possible for us to look forward

81

to death as we anticipate entering into the presence of our Lord.

As Adoniram Judson, famous missionary to Burma, lay dying, he called out: "I go with the gladness of a boy bounding away from school. I feel strong in God."

As Christians we can face death with courage, not because we want to escape life, but because we want to enter into it more fully. Our desire will be expressed not with a mournful sigh, but with a confident hope. And if we question whether this actually can become so, we may be assured that this miracle of a changed attitude can come about because of God's unlimited and unrestricted grace, a grace God stands ready to give freely.

O Lord, rid my heart of all vain anxieties and paralyzing fears. Give me a cheerful and buoyant spirit, and peace in doing your will, for Christ's sake.

—John Baillie

What If?

Everything I fear and dread comes true (3:25).

For the thing that I fear comes upon me,
and what I dread befalls me (3:25, RSV).

Had Job, even in his years of plenty, occasionally laid awake at night, plagued by the "what ifs"?

What if a plague strikes and wipes out my herds of sheep?

What if my camels are stolen?

What if our crops fail?

What if our children fall victim to a deadly disease and die?

"I knew things were going too well for them to continue," we can almost hear him say now.

Mercifully, everything we fear does not happen to us. We are told that 99 percent of our fears never materialize. This is the discovery Job will make. How foolish, then, to waste energy worrying about that which by 100:1 odds may never happen! And even if the trouble comes, God will give us the grace to bear it.

Men never do evil so completely and cheerfully as when they do it from religious conviction.

—Blaise Pascal

All mischief begins in the name of God.

—A German Proverb

Who Is in Control?

Your wickedness is evident by what you say . . . . A wicked man who oppresses others will be in torment as long as he lives. . . . fire will destroy the homes built by bribery (15:5, 20, 34). (Insinuation that Job is wicked, has oppressed others, and is guilty of bribery.)

That is the man . . . who seized houses whose owners had fled (15:28). (Direct attack against Job.)

He will not remain rich for long . . . . Before his time is up he will wither . . . . There will be no descendants for godless men (15:29, 32, 34). (Threats of further disaster for Job.)

Put away evil . . . . [then] your life will be brighter than sunshine at noon (11:14,17). (Promises and rewards.)

Job's friends believed in cause and effect—you reap what you sow. They also believe that God rewards the righteous but punishes evildoers. Therefore, they were sure that Job's troubles were a clear indication that he had sinned. They came to set their friend right, to urge him to repent, to see him restored to a right relationship with God. They even felt God had called them to do this. "We have spoken for him [God] with calm, even words," they declared (15:11).

As we read the conversations of Job's friends, we shall see that in order to persuade Job to do what they wanted— to "repent"—his friends used four techniques.

1. By *insinuation* they sowed seeds of doubt as to his standing with God. They repeatedly accused him of not being right with God.

2. By *direct attack and accusation* they damaged his name and character and bruised his self-esteem.

3. By *threatening* they sought to intimidate him.

4. By *offering tantalizing rewards* they tried to entice and lure him.

As we read the Book of Job we must always remember that Satan is behind Job's temptations. He is working through Job's friends; their techniques are those the evil one has used from the beginning.

In the Garden with Adam and Eve, Satan *raised doubts by asking questions.*

"Did God say . . . ?" he taunted. He insinuated both that what God had said was not really true and that God was not a loving, just God. He questioned God's word and God's character.

The scribes from Jerusalem *accused* Jesus of being possessed by Beelzebul, another name for Satan. What a turnabout this was—Satan's encouraging people to identify God's Son as Satan so others would turn away from Him!

Peter felt the sting of *direct attack* the night of Jesus' betrayal as he stood warming himself at a brazier of coals and a young girl accused him of being one of Jesus' followers. To have been identified with Christ on that night would have thrown Peter into a dangerous position indeed. Satan was "sifting him as wheat."

Rewards were dangled in front of Eve's eyes. "If you eat this fruit, you will be like God," Satan promised. Satan likewise offered Jesus rewards and power in the kingdoms of this world if Jesus would worship him.

As you study the conversations of Job's friends, you may find it enlightening to note in the margins when they used these techniques by writing "insinuation," "false accusation," "threat," and "reward offered."

Also, be on the alert for another characteristic of their speech, which we have mentioned before. Truth and falsehood are intertwined. This both deceives and confuses. Even we as readers can be confused as we read the account if we are not aware of this element.

Job's drama is very ancient, but it portrays tactics used even today by people who seek to control others. Satan deludes some of them into believing they are acting on God's behalf when they try to control others. They forget that each of us individually and directly is responsible to God for our attitudes and actions.

True, we seek the counsel and guidance of Christian brothers and sisters, but we should let no one but the Holy Spirit control us.

The "patience of Job" is struggle all the way, the patience of one who grapples with apparent contradictions and wrests his comfort from painful paradox.

Gerhard E. Frost

Planting Sugar Cane, Reaping Horseradish

Job, will you be annoyed if I speak? . . . You have taught many people and given strength to feeble hands. . . . Now it's your turn to be in trouble, and you are too stunned to face it. You worshiped God, and your life was blameless; and so you should have confidence and hope. Think back now. Name a single case where a righteous man met with disaster. I have seen people plow fields of evil and plant wickedness like seed; now they harvest wickedness and evil (4:1-8).

Eliphaz—the oldest, the most pious, dignified, sympathetic, courteous, learned, wise, and eloquent of Job's friends—now speaks.

He begins kindly. "Job, will you be annoyed if I speak?" he asks.

Because our text does not reveal how Eliphaz was feeling at this point and because tone of voice cannot be conveyed in written dialogue, we do not really know how to interpret Eliphaz's next words. Was he appealing to Job's past praiseworthy efforts in order to encourage him to continue to stand fast? Or was he speaking sarcastically when he said, "You have taught many people . . . . Now it's your turn to be in trouble, and you are too stunned to face it"?

By his next words, however, Eliphaz intimates, for the first of many times to follow, that if Job's life really had been blameless, all this trouble wouldn't have happened to him. "What you sow, you will reap," he says flatly.

In this case, however, Job is reaping what he did not sow.

When my husband and I lived in Africa, we learned of a trick farmers employed to get even with an enemy. At seedtime, when the ground was soft and receptive because it had just been cultivated, on a dark night a farmer would slip over to an enemy's field and sow seeds of weeds and thistles. Only much later did his work become evident, and then digging out the weeds and thistles demanded much backbreaking, perspiring work. Anger and resentment simmered within the victim.

This practice evidently is centuries old, for Jesus referred to it in the parable of the tares.

So Eliphaz's insinuation that Job's trouble has come upon him because of disobedience to God is a glib answer. As we know, an enemy has been at work.

It is a fallacy to believe that if we try to serve God and walk with Him we shall be spared trouble and all will go well for us. Dick Dugan, writing in *Decision* magazine, tells how for 14 years he had believed that no evil could befall those who had surrendered to Christ. But one day a tornado picked up the cabin he and his family were in and catapulted them into a lake. Miraculously, he survived as a 20-foot wall of water crashed over him. When the storm ceased, he picked himself up and went in search of his family. He found his wife, big with a child to whom she gave birth two months later, and two of their children. But their five-year-old daughter, Sharon, had disappeared. Three days later they found her in 50 feet of water, partly hidden under the branches of a large tree.

Through it all "I have learned," Dugan stated, "that I am no exception to either the blessings or the buffets of life. I can praise God . . . in all things and take pleasure in infirmities, but I know I will not be exempted."

Sorry, Eliphaz, but what you are telling your friend Job isn't entirely true. We do not reap only what we sow.

My dear friends, do not believe all who claim to
have the Spirit, but test them to find out if the
spirit they have is from God.

—1 John 4:1

Testing Mystical Experiences

> Once a message came quietly, so quietly I could
> hardly hear it. . . . A light breeze touched my face,
> and my skin crawled with fright. I could see some-
> thing standing there; I stared, but couldn't tell
> what it was. Then I heard a voice out of the silence
> . . . (4:12, 15, 16).

Eastern peoples, for whom the spirit world is more real
than it is for us Westerners, frequently have testified to mystical appearances. Today, however, even a number of West-
ern Christians claim to see visions and hear God speak.

Eliphaz had been thrilled with such a visitation. He
shares it now with Job. But as many others after him have
done, Eliphaz makes the mistake of embracing as doctrinal
truth what he claims to have heard, without testing to see
if it is indeed true.

Even as the truth in isolated Bible verses must be
checked against the whole teaching of the Word of God,
so must mystical experiences be examined carefully. Satan
can deceive through mystical experiences. Check out how

many cults have had their birth in their founder's claims of having received special revelations from God.

Even today, certain Christian leaders drift from biblical teaching and expose themselves to error when they question whether God's Word is His final revelation to us. "Why cannot God continue to speak new truths to us through revelation and prophecy?" they ask. Questions like that remind me of a childhood experience.

In the spring of the year in Minnesota, ponds frequently are thinly covered with what we call "rubber ice." When we were children, walking on "rubber ice" was a scary, thrilling, daring adventure. It would dip and bend under us, and we had to keep moving quickly to prevent its breaking under us. To seek further revelations from God to add to the teachings of the Bible is like walking on "rubber ice." Sooner or later the ice will break.

A pastor went to his wife one day and announced that an angel had appeared to him and commanded him to leave her and take as his wife the wife of another man in their congregation. The woman in question claimed that the angel had appeared to her also.

Another Christian man had severed relationships with his wife and was living with the wife of another. When reprimanded for his action, he retorted, "Whom are we to obey—God or man? God has told us to live this way."

Rubbish! God never tells His people to sin, and to forsake one's spouse to cleave to the spouse of another is sin.

Mystical revelations must always be checked against the Word of God; His revelation, which we find in the Bible, is sufficient and final.

As we consider mystical experiences, it is helpful to ask another question. What has happened in one's life and heart as a result of the experience?

Eliphaz's speeches reveal him to be dogmatic, rigid, judgmental, and lacking in understanding. Eliphaz preached at Job. He scolded him. He also talked about God, while Job talked to God.

Mystical experiences, tingling and exciting though they may be, need to pass the scrutiny of the Bible, while at the same time give evidence of producing a more tender, understanding acceptance of others.

God does not only love all men in general, but each of us in particular.

— Paul Tournier

Every situation is distinguished by its uniqueness.

— Viktor Frankl

If I Were You

If I were you . . . (5:8).

David Grayson, in his book *Adventures of Solitude*, makes this observation: "The hospital diagnoses before it prescribes; the church often prescribes before it diagnoses."

Eliphaz, who hasn't begun to "hear Job out," who hasn't listened in order to understand what really is troubling Job, is ready to prescribe a remedy for him.

How often trite answers spring to our lips, declarations of the doctrines we have been taught! We have not learned to stand in awe and questioning before the uniqueness of each individual's hurt. We think "four spiritual laws," properly applied, taped in place, and prayed over will automatically bring every person to faith in Jesus Christ. Likewise, we think quoting certain Bible verses will restore or strengthen faith or answer questions and alleviate doubt.

What will it take to teach us to approach each person with humility and a teachable spirit so that we are willing to spend the time needed to make the right diagnosis and prescribe the right treatment?

Eliphaz evidently was so sure he had the right answers he didn't stop to question what he was going to say. And, after all, his first words seemed so right, how could they be wrong? "If I were you," he said to Job, "I would turn to God."

But the words, "If I were you," are some of the easiest words to utter.

"If I were you, I wouldn't try to have any more children; God evidently doesn't want you to have any."

"If I were you, I would be thankful it was my baby who died, not my husband."

"If I were you, I would be thankful God took my baby; maybe he wouldn't have been right anyway."

"If I had children . . . If my son didn't want to work . . . If I couldn't get along with my spouse . . . If I had your job . . . "

"If I were you . . . " Eliphaz says. How does he know what he would do? He isn't in Job's situation. He hasn't been bereaved of all his children. He hasn't lost his home or gone bankrupt. He doesn't have cancer—or probably even a headache.

Yet how quickly and glibly we make similar remarks! A businessman, struggling with a difficult, vexing problem, tries to share it with his wife. She responds with an easy solution and implies he is a dumbbell not to have figured out an answer. Is that husband likely to continue to share with her the problems that churn in his mind?

Bishop Hans Lilje, writing about his time in a German concentration camp in the 1940s, shares what a horrible discovery it was for him to experience real hunger.

"Hunger attacked us with elemental force like a strong man armed, who throws you to the ground," he writes. "Until now I did not know that hunger makes everything go black before your eyes, and that you can only rise from your bed with the greatest difficulty to totter across the room."

94

I wonder if Eliphaz, visiting Bishop Lilje in his prison cell, would have said, "I know just how you feel when you're hungry. If I were you . . . "

Or if he would say that to the 200,000 who subsist on the sidewalks of Calcutta.

Job didn't need an Eliphaz to say, "If I were you . . . I know just how you feel." Rather, he needed an arm around his shoulder, hands to help rebuild his demolished house, money to replenish his lost herds, and patient acceptance and understanding as he struggled with his own grief and personal conflict with God.

And our suffering world needs the same.

A Christian is nothing but a sinful person who has put himself or herself to school with Christ for the honest purpose of becoming better.

— Henry Ward Beecher

Can Chastisement Be Good?

Happy is the person whom God corrects! Do not resent it when he rebukes you. God bandages the wounds he makes; his hand hurts you, and his hand heals (5:17, 18).

Several years ago, when my brother Carl tumbled wearily into bed on a hot July night in the Midwest, he had no premonition that within 24 hours his arms would be dangling uselessly by his side. Around midnight, racking pains in his shoulders awakened him.

"Can it be an attack of acute arthritis?" he wondered, easing himself out of bed. He paced. The pain intensified. He dropped stiffly into the rocking chair and rocked. The agonizing pain grayed his face. Perspiration drenched him. By morning, both arms hung limp and useless at his sides.

A trip to the hospital was the preface to weeks of prolonged tests, increased pain, and lengthy hospital stays. Finally, doctors at Mayo Clinic diagnosed his disease as "acute bilateral brachial plexitis," a rare nerve disease for which no treatment was known.

96

When the disease burned itself out, it left Carl with two useless arms. Unable to care for his dairy herd, he had no choice but to sell them. He wept the day the big trucks hauled them away. Then, in his bedroom of their home, on the now-quiet farm with the empty barns, he began therapy. More agony followed as atrophied muscles cried out in protest against being forced into use. Slowly, progress was made. A year passed. He persisted with his painful therapy.

Months later, registered cows with bulging udders, warm animal smells, and muted mooings filled Carl's barns. His right arm had grown muscular and strong again. His left arm filled a supportive role. Adaptations in machinery compensated for his weakened left arm.

Looking back on the testing, Carl and his wife, Lorraine, regard it as a chastisement from the Lord.

"Things had gone so well for us that we had become quite self-sufficient. Now we were cast on God, and we had to reassess our lives and reexamine our values."

"I had been complaining bitterly about all the work a farm demands of its owners," Lorraine confessed. "Suddenly Carl couldn't work at all. I was working harder than ever and discovering that work is a great blessing."

"Probably because our family always had been so well and strong, we never really had been able to understand why so many people were sick so much, nor did we sympathize with them really," Carl added. He laughed ruefully. "I used to speak with disparaging pity about people who got sick. Now we were discovering how uncertain life is, how within a matter of hours and even minutes we can become more helpless than a baby."

"I think we accepted what happened," Lorraine said, "because we believe our heavenly Father loves us dearly and that He is interested in shaping our lives into the image of His Son. Not once were we tempted to wonder whether or not God had forsaken us. Instead, we actually felt God had been kind to us."

Ernest Gordon shares a conversation he had with a fellow prisoner of war when at last, at the end of World War II, they were on a ship bound for England. Gordon was musing at the ship's rail when he noticed John Leckie standing next to him.

"Well," John said, "it's all over. I wouldn't have missed it for anything. True, it was rough. But I learned an awful lot that I couldn't have learned at university or anywhere else. For one, I've learned about the things of life that are real and for another, I've learned it's great to be alive."

"It was easy for me to see how he could make such a remark," Gordon states. "The experiences we had passed through deepened our understanding of life and of each other. We had looked into the heart of the Eternal and found him to be wonderfully kind."

And the change that was wrought in these men through their years of suffering was lasting. Gordon notes that after they re-entered civilian life, some studied for the ministry. Others became teachers, welfare officers, research technicians, or doctors. One doctor serves a coal-mining community in Wales. One works in the field of virus diseases. Another man uses his artistic skills in cartoons designed to provoke thought. In addition to their daily professions and jobs they have helped build orphanages and hospitals and have supported welfare work.

"On the whole," Gordon notes, "they appear to have made much more of a success of their lives in the difficult postwar period than those who had an easier time of it . . . . Their marriages have been more lasting. . . . And statistics cannot tell us much of fears overcome, of aspirations realized, of the seeds of faith, hope, and love which lodged in their hearts to flower later in the lives of others."

The benefits Carl and Lorraine, Ernest Gordon, and his fellow prisoners of war received from their difficult experiences resulted largely because of their teachable attitudes.

In contrast, a proud, independent spirit can prevent us from receiving what we should when God chastises us.

Once when I was being severely tested and, I thought, being unjustly treated, a friend wrote: "It wouldn't hurt to ask God what He wants to teach you through this." But I was too resentful and angry and too proud to be willing to bend and pray such a prayer. As a result, the benefits I finally gained from the experience were delayed a number of years.

God does chastise His children. But chastisement is different from punishment, although Job's friends confused the two. Punishment is retributive, inflicting a penalty upon us for something we have done wrong. God's chastisement is corrective, designed to purify us, bring us back to Him, and enable us to live more effectively for Him in the future. Because of this, we can thank God when He chastises us.

If we believe in Jesus, it is not what we gain, but what He pours through us that counts. It is not that God makes us beautifully rounded grapes, but that He squeezes the sweetness out of us. Spiritually, we cannot measure our life by success, but only by what God pours through us, and we cannot measure that at all.

— Oswald Chambers

Think Mink?

The fields you plow will be free of rocks . . . (see 5:19-27).

Eliphaz assures Job that if he will accept his trials as discipline from the Lord, then nothing but success will be sure to follow. In today's setting we could paraphrase Eliphaz's glowing promises this way:

You will be safe when you drive on the freeways, and even though recession comes, your investments will escape undepleted in value.

Though wars break out and you are drafted into service, you will be assigned a safe desk position.

Your condominium will be behind locked gates, guaranteeing you security from robbers,

and in your affluent country, people will not have to stand in bread lines.

Your investments in bonds and real estate will net you huge profits,

100

and in business no dishonest people will fleece you.

You will meet the man or girl of your dreams who will love you forever.

Your children will be born strong and healthy, and only as many and as close together as you want them, and your wife will give birth to them in relaxed, easy, natural child birth at home, and without any complications, and you assisting.

You yourself will enjoy vigorous health, a youthful figure, a thrilling sex life, and sharp intellect even in your declining years, with continuing promotions and salary raises, and your end shall be like the resplendent setting of the sun in the west.

Glorious, isn't it? Who doesn't want a life like that?

Certain groups in the Christian community today hold out these alluring promises to listeners. "God never meant for you to be poor." "God doesn't want you to be sick." "God means for you to succeed." "Think mink."

So-called Christian books offer us secrets about how we can succeed personally, financially, socially, spiritually, physically, corporately, and intellectually.

This was the message Job's friends were repeating to him. But having just suffered reversals of every kind, their bright words and smiling faces and positive statements only deepened Job's depression.

In contrast to the promises held out by Job's friends, how different the words of Jesus sound:

"The world will make you suffer" (John 16:33).

"Whosoever does not take up his cross and follow in my steps is not fit to be my disciple" (Matt. 10:38).

"Whoever tries to gain his own life will lose it; but whoever loses his life for my sake will gain it" (Matt. 10:39).

Eliphaz, your promises to Job are not God's promises. He has never promised us unchallenged, unfailing success.

101

He has never promised us trouble- and disease-free lives. He has promised to see us through whatever comes. But there's a vast difference between the two. Eliphaz, and all you who seek to counsel and teach people, be true as you declare to people what God promises them.

Creating unrealistic—and even non-Christian—appetites and desires in others can produce disastrous and tragic results. We can portray sex and marriage as bringing the ultimate pleasure and satisfaction and thus lead people to expect the impossible from married life. Disillusionment, discontent, unreasonable expectations, and dissatisfaction develop because "I am not getting out of my marriage all I had hoped to," and these self-centered, selfish expectations can lead to divorce.

Being lured and urged by companies to work harder and harder to procure raises and bonuses and promotions can lead to a sterile life, empty and cold because there has been time only for company interests and no time to develop meaningful relationships.

Colorful, scientifically conceived ads can make us want this product and that product until our lives become engrossed in accumulating a microwave oven, a powerful status car, and a bathtub in the backyard. But in the end we shall find ourselves not grateful and cheerful, but complaining and dissatisfied, because things satisfy only for a short time. Some of us never seem to learn this lesson.

Working for top academic degrees can isolate us from our families and cause us to rationalize away our responsibilities to them. With little time for communication, family members become strangers to each other. Basic needs of the heart are not met.

Jesus taught that love brings meaning to life, and love finds many forms and expressions. But how popular would the appeal be if our sermons and articles and books showed us how we can sacrifice in order to love, how we can seek the happiness of others and not our own?

No, Eliphaz's personal success philosophy is easy to listen to—until we get sick, fail an exam, break out with acne, get hurt in a love affair, lose a promotion, our children get stoned with drugs or drunk with alcohol, we face a divorce, or we shiver through a winter or line up for gasoline.

Then, suddenly, Eliphaz's promises echo with hollowness. But how sad that until that happens we continue to welcome and promote his success philosophy.

It is not miserable to be blind; it is miserable to be incapable of enduring blindness.

— John Milton

Do I Have a Choice?

I have no appetite for food like that, and everything I eat makes me sick. . . . What strength do I have to keep on living? Why go on living when I have no hope? Am I made of stones? Is my body bronze? . . . Month after month I have nothing to live for; night after night brings me grief (6:7, 11, 12; 7:3).

To face, articulate, and finally to accept our disappointments and losses is one of the most difficult tasks the human psyche faces," believes Dr. Roy Menninger, president of The Menninger Foundation. However, if we can realize that even in our losses we are offered some choices, our suffering becomes more endurable.

Job has not yet realized that he does have some choices. "I have nothing to live for," he complains. Graphically he describes his feelings: his lack of appetite, the almost paralyzing sense of hopelessness, his feeling of not being able to endure any more. He wishes he could stop living, that he could escape.

But he can't, and neither can we when times get tough.

A young girl whose engagement had just been broken said sadly, "I wish I wasn't me."

A popular song of some years ago used to plead, "Stop the world, I want to get off."

But we're on, and even if the world isn't always pleasant, we can't get off. We either have to accept things as they are or make them better. We have no choice but to bear the risks of being here, but we do have the choice of determining what suffering will do to us.

Life is a gift, the most precious gift we have. But life has a price also. Life brings pain and suffering, disappointment and loss, as well as joy and rewards, success and happiness. We must be prepared to accept both.

The world is not a place of guaranteed security; rather, it is a world with brave people. The pages of Scripture are full of stories, not only about people who succeeded and prospered, but about brave people who faced whatever life brought them. They either failed because they chose to bear it alone, or they triumphed in the midst of pain, suffering, loss, betrayal, and failure because they chose to avail themselves of God's help.

My friend Magdalene Lange, in the midst of deep suffering, learned that she had this choice. After learning that her husband, Bob, had two, or at the most three, years to live, she was too shocked to think. Then she fell into his arms, and they both cried. The doctors had told Bob that he had acute amyotrophic lateral sclerosis, a rare nerve disease, more commonly known as Lou Gehrig's disease.

Bob and Magdalene made some preliminary plans. They made out their wills, put their financial affairs in order, and arranged for the care of their two children in the event both of them died. This done, Magdalene admits that unconsciously she blocked out the reality of Bob's condition. As long as he could work, this wasn't too difficult. But when visible deteriorations became more frequent and serious, she found anger welling up.

Eventually she and Bob heard of a new experimental drug being used in Houston, and Bob volunteered to test the drug. A friend stopped in as Magdalene was packing Bob's suitcase. She remarked how good it was Bob could go to Texas. Suddenly Magdalene erupted. "We've no choice, have we?" she exploded, blinking her eyes rapidly.

Once she had framed in spoken word the gnawing, tormenting question, it began to haunt her at every corner. It echoed and reechoed in her ears: "You have no choice. You have no choice." Defiantly she began to voice it more and more frequently, bitterness tinging her remarks.

Bob bore patiently with her. "Let's sing," he would say. Or he would gently tease her. But Magdalene's tension continued to build.

"I felt so helpless and frustrated as I watched the paralysis creep slowly upward until Bob could move only his head," Magdalene admits. "Here was an alive, vibrant man trapped in his own body, only 41 years old, at the peak of his productivity but doomed."

She wandered aimlessly around his bedroom one day, arranging the lampshade, straightening the books, picking lint from the rug. And then suddenly she was pounding the wall, hot tears scalding her cheeks.

"We've no choice!" she complained.

"Wrong!" Bob's voice from the bed spun her around. "It is true," his words were deliberate, "that our situation cannot be changed. More often than not in life, situations cannot be changed." He paused to rest. Breathing was becoming increasingly difficult for him. "Blessings come to us," he went on, forging out every word, "and sometimes tragedy. But that does not mean we do not have a choice. We always have a choice. Sometimes our choices may be limited. For us, circumstances have funneled our choices down now to only two." He paused. "We can accept what has come and trust God to work for good, or we can become bitter and rebel and thereby destroy not only ourselves but all around us. But we have a choice. Remember, Magdalene, we always have a choice."

106

"I fell to my knees by his bed," Magdalene recalls. "I laid my hands on Bob's wasted body and hid my face in the folds of the bedclothes and sobbed. We did have choices, I realized. We had had choices, and we had made wise, good choices.

"We had chosen, first of all, to believe our doctor's diagnosis and had been thankful for time to prepare. We had put everything in order. We had chosen to continue work as long as both of us could. To enable Bob to work we had installed the chair lift, fitted the car so he could drive, procured leg braces, crutches, page turner, respirator, anything that would help. We had chosen not to resign to fate, but had explored healing possibilities. We had chosen to share our struggles and victories so this crisis experience would be a learning experience for our families, neighbors, and friends, rather than choosing to remain tight-lipped and silent."

All this Magdalene recalled as she knelt at Bob's bed. Her sobs subsided. New strength came. She did have choices, she realized. She could accept this testing in its ultimate, final form and let it purify and refine her. This assurance brought peace.

Magdalene realized that indeed we always do have a choice, and our choice will affect not only us but others. But Job has not stumbled upon or accepted this yet. All he wants to do is die.

Give me control of my thoughts, if I should
lie awake. Give me grace, if as I lie abed I think at
all, to think upon Thee.

— John Baillie

I Can't Sleep!

When I lie down to sleep, the hours drag; I toss
all night and long for dawn. . . . I lie down and
try to rest; I look for relief from my pain. But you—
you terrify me with dreams; you send me visions
and nightmares (7:4, 13, 14).

Vividly, Job describes the nightmares and sleeplessness
caused by shock. Some doctors believe that 85 percent of
those who suffer from severe loss encounter sleep problems.

We know that when tension mounts to stress, we need
to give even more careful attention to the needs of our
bodies—to exercise, good diet, and more rest than usual.
But what can we do if rest is difficult to get?

For months after our first little son was born and died,
I relived that experience in torturous dreams. I gave birth
to that baby dozens of times.

Some years later I again experienced this reliving of a
tragic incident. I was driving downtown Los Angeles when
a car sped out from an alleyway. I saw it coming, as in slow
motion. I knew we would collide, but with cars parked on
both sides of the narrow streets there wasn't a thing I could
do. The sharp sound of crumpling steel and shattering glass
as my car was pushed over against a parked car, the stillness

that followed when motion ceased—all these remain vividly imprinted on my memory. The next recollection was feeling something warm stream down my face, putting my hand up, withdrawing it and seeing blood, and realizing that I was injured.

For months following that accident I relived it in dreams, usually gripped with paralyzing fear as, in my dream, my foot was so heavy I could not move it from accelerator to brake. I would wake up clutching my leg, trying to pull it off the accelerator.

I later found out that some terrifying dreams can trigger movements so violent we could injure ourselves in our sleep. So to protect us from this, our brain sends messages to our muscles, actually paralyzing us so we cannot move. After I understood this, my emotional distress was eased.

And although the dreams were terrifying, I eventually learned to recognize their value and accept them. It was as though the only way the impact of the shock could be dulled was for me to relive the experience over and over. I compared it to developing a callous so I would be able to use my hands at hard labor without blisters or pain.

I also learned that sedatives, barbiturates, tranquilizers, and alcohol suppress dreams, and that among alcoholics continuous suppression of dreams can produce delirium tremors.

So dreams can be beneficial and healing, and when my attitude toward the dreams changed from one of dread to one of acceptance, I no longer woke up perspiring, and the dreams became less and less frequent.

Job also refers to the problem of sleeplessness. How well some of us are acquainted with this, too. Either we are unable to drop off to sleep or we wake up at two or three in the morning and can't get back to sleep.

A word of caution needs to be said about the use of sleeping pills, barbiturates, and tranquilizers. At present they are the most frequently prescribed drugs today, enough to provide every man, woman, and child in the United States with 20 a year. In contrast, antibiotics run a poor second.

There are times when these drugs may be needed and should be used, but only when reliable doctors who really care about their patients prescribe them. Nor should we coax or cajole a doctor into prescribing them. They are too easily tempted to write a prescription for Valium or some other sedative. A large percentage of patients in doctors' offices are there not because of any organic breakdown, but because of a psychosomatic problem which, in turn, affects their bodies. Doctors recognize this, but either they consider themselves unqualified to deal with such problems, or they simply cannot take the time. The easiest solution is to prescribe a tranquilizer.

But tranquilizers simply postpone confronting whatever is troubling a person. And they can be addictive.

Barbara Gordon, in her book *I'm Dancing As Fast As I Can*, tells of how she began to take Valium after she injured her back in college. Later, her work as a documentary film producer and writer often built tensions to intolerable levels, and she turned to Valium to relieve the pressures. Her last documentary was about a woman dying of cancer, and when the woman died, Barbara suddenly was motivated to live her own life to the fullest. She decided to go off Valium.

No one warned her, however, about Valium withdrawal. Her scalp seemed to be on fire; her brain sizzled. Her hands trembled so she couldn't pick up a cup of coffee. Her nervousness increased. Unable to function, she would sit for days, unbathed and unable to dress herself. Severe headaches almost drove her mad, and finally delirium and convulsions set in. It took more than three years, 20 doctors, her career, five months of treatment in an insane asylum, and medical bills totaling more than $150,000 before she realized full recovery. It is clear that sedatives and tranquilizers should be used only in moments of real crisis, and then in very limited dosages.

But what shall we do if we can't sleep without them?

Perhaps a change of attitude is more important. My aged mother, who slept poorly for a number of years, was philosophical about it.

"My body rests even if I am not actually asleep," she insisted. How else could we children explain the energy of an 85-year-old woman who planted and cared for gardens and berry patches in spite of arthritis and heart problems?

Mother didn't fight her sleeplessness. She used her wakeful hours to marvel at the night sky. She thrilled to the racing, mysterious beauty of the Northern Lights. She knew the path of the moon. Mother enjoyed many nighttime wonders that most of us miss.

Those who are periodically troubled with wakefulness should experiment to learn what will help. A glass of hot milk. Exercise before bed (but not strenuous exercise). A warm (not hot) bath. Quitting work an hour before bedtime and doing something relaxing. Getting up and reading for half an hour if one awakens and cannot get back to sleep. Trying a different bed. Repeating Bible verses. Recalling peaceful scenes. Reading poetry. Listening to peaceful music. And short naps during the day to compensate for sleeplessness at night. The most important thing is not to worry about it. We can get along with comparatively little sleep.

So when we, like Job, experience sleep problems, we need not worry. This phase too, like all the others, will pass.

111

If you have the whine in you, kick it out ruthlessly.
It is a positive crime to be weak in God's strength.
— Oswald Chambers

Poor Me!

> Soon I will be in my grave, and I'll be gone when
> you look for me (7:21).

I was just a little girl and my mother had spanked me—for what, I can't remember. Then she had banished me to the playroom, next to our kitchen. I was lying on the couch sobbing my heart out, not because of the mild stinging discomfort on my bottom, but because I envisioned myself lying in a coffin, white and still. Mother was bending over me, weeping and exclaiming in remorse, "And the last thing I did was spank her." The mere thought affected me greatly, and in deep pity for myself I sobbed.

Job too, momentarily, slips into a childish reaction.

"You're so mean to me, God," he complains, wagging his finger at God. And then he bursts out, "If You keep this up, I'll soon be in my grave, and then You'll be sorry!"

Self-pity is one of the most frequent and enticing temptations that come to us in trouble. "Poor, poor me! I really have it hard! God's really been tough on me!"

Bob Lange's wife, Magdalene, shared with me the struggle she had with self-pity the three years Bob was slowly dying from Lou Gehrig's disease.

"But Bob would never tolerate it," she said. "I remember the time he had been hospitalized with a blood

112

clot. I was doing dishes and crying into the sink. I cried into the morning paper. I cried in the chapel when I got down to the hospital. And when I walked into Bob's room, I cried again.

"The orderly was giving Bob his bath. Bob was lying on his stomach with his head turned to the side. He looked at me as I came sobbing to his bedside.

" 'Well, well,' he said. 'Here is Magdalene spooning out a little self-pity for herself.'

"I started to laugh, and then I was laughing and crying at the same time until finally I was all laughed out and cried out."

Job has no one to help him stiffen his back, laugh away his self-pity, or direct his pity toward others. So he continues to voice his death wish as he periodically pours little trickles of self-pity over himself.

"If we give way to self-pity and indulge in the luxury of misery, we banish God's riches from our own lives and hinder others from entering into His provision," Oswald Chambers states. "Self-pity obliterates God and puts self-interest on the throne. It opens our mouths to spit out murmurings and our lives become craving spiritual sponges; there is nothing lovely or generous about them."

When our desires are thwarted and life becomes
too much for us, it is easy to reject life and the
pain it brings, easier to die than to live.

— Ernest Gordon

Sometimes We Have to Get Angry

... I am angry ... I have to speak (7:11).

As Job sits submerged in self-pity, suddenly there is a change. Anger flares up within him—deep, resentful anger.

"No!" he shouts, "I can't be quiet! I am angry and bitter, and I have to speak."

This marks a significant turning point in Job's recovery. If the suffering one collapses in apathy and surrenders to the desire to die, there is little hope for recovery.

Viktor Frankl, commenting on his work in the hospital of a German concentration camp, notes in his book *Man's Search for Meaning*:

> Apathy was particularly increased among the feverish patients, so that they did not react unless they were shouted at. Even this failed at times, and then it took tremendous self-control not to strike them. For one's own irritability took on enormous proportions in the face of the other's apathy and especially in the face of danger (i.e., the approaching inspection) which was caused by it.

114

Frankl also observed that without faith in the future and a will to live, bodies fell victim to illness. When hope is gone, people die.

My husband and I were 30 when we were married—a highly advanced age, we thought at the time. Our parental instinct was strong; we wanted children very much. But two sons were born to us prematurely, and they both died. Our doctor shook his head. Considering the anxious months of threatened trouble that had preceded the tragic losses, he questioned whether I would ever be able to give birth to a fully developed, strong, healthy baby.

I was plunged into despair. It seemed such a useless waste! All the potential for two beautiful, meaningful lives lay in those two bodies, but it was a potential that could never be developed. I saw no hope for the future.

I began to shake with chills. Then I drenched my bed with sweat as a raging fever shot through me. Alarmed and perplexed, the doctors ran a battery of tests. It was no use; they could not pinpoint the cause of my soaring temperature.

In the meantime, I lay limp and uncaring. I was so depressed I was ready to welcome any end to my suffering and sorrow.

Then my doctor strode into the room. Standing by my bed, he began to needle and taunt me. Astonished, and not believing what I was hearing, I sat up. Anger began to surge within. How dare he talk to me that way! How dare he accuse me of bringing the fever on myself! How dare he blame me for being selfish and cowardly and not loving my husband!

I lashed back at him. He listened for a while, unprotesting, then wheeled around and walked from the room.

That night my temperature returned to normal. My anger was the reality of how I felt inside; it was my turning point to continue on.

115

So the introduction here of Job's anger is a hopeful turning point. Job is roused from his stupor of despair and his death wish. We can look now for the beginning of his recovery—rocky though it will be!

A friend is someone who knows you're not perfect, but loves you anyway.

What Kind of a Friend Are You?

> In trouble like this I need loyal friends—whether I've forsaken God or not (6:14).

Job continues to spill out his anguish and anger, tinged deeply with despair and hopelessness.

Job says to God:

> Is it right for you to be so cruel? . . .
>
> Your hands formed and shaped me, and now those same hands destroy me. . . . You have given me life and constant love, and your care has kept me alive. But now I know that all the time you were secretly planning to harm me. You were watching to see if I would sin, so that you could refuse to forgive me. As soon as I sin, I'm in trouble with you, but when I do right, I get no credit. . . . If I have any success at all, you hunt me down like a lion. . . .
>
> Why, God, did you let me be born? . . . Leave me alone! I am going soon and will never come back— going to a land that is dark and gloomy, a land of darkness, shadows, and confusion, where the light is darkness (Job 10:3, 8, 12-16, 18, 20-22).

It's uncomfortable to listen to people who explode in anger, especially when they act in what seems an extreme and inappropriate manner. But people who have been severely hurt need someone who will act as a buffer.

I was talking on the phone one day when the operator cut in with an emergency call from a hospital. The five-year-old son of a young woman friend had been struck by a car and hurled into the air and was seriously injured. Could I come?

We found the boy's mother—we'll call her Susan—in the tiny waiting room in the emergency ward, sitting bolt upright on the edge of her chair, brown eyes huge and wide with fright. A couple of years earlier her husband had disappeared. She had been left to care for their three small children. Tim, as we shall call the five-year-old, was very strong-willed and hard to manage. Susan often had expressed her fears about how she would be able to raise him.

Three hours later, a doctor and a nurse hustled us off to a small staff sitting room and shut the door. Gently the doctor said, "Your child didn't make it."

Susan didn't comprehend.

"Your child is dead."

Susan turned on me then and bit my arms and pounded my chest with her fists.

"I can't believe it! I must see him!"

They led us to the emergency room, where a sheet covered the still little figure on the table. Susan threw off the sheet and bent over the figure, caressing it, talking to it, trying to coax a response. When there was none, she threw herself to the floor and tried to pound her head against the floor.

"I want to die! God, I hate you!" she screamed.

I got down on the floor beside her and tried to keep her from hitting her head on the tile. She fought me and thrashed about. I crept along beside her as she moved across the room. Finally she lunged at me, crawled up into my lap

118

like a very frightened child, buried her nose in my breast, and began to sob quietly. Slowly I felt her body relax and she became quiet. Immense grief and sorrow still consumed her, but the strongest force of her anger and fright had drained away.

To experience anger and fright following severe loss is not uncommon or unnatural. The anger may erupt for many reasons—because we feel threatened or cheated or guilty for having caused the death. The anger may be expressed violently and explosively, or in a menacingly quiet statement that barely betrays the pressure-cooker forces building within.

Job exploded and trusted his friends enough to react before them honestly. But they could not handle it.

"Will no one answer all this nonsense?" cries Zophar, the youngest friend, and he proceeds to castigate Job (11:1).

We listen with disbelief to Zophar's statements, finding it hard to believe that a person can be as insensitive and unfeeling as he is. Opinionated, bigoted, and unrestrained, he states his position emphatically and authoritatively and puts a big black exclamation point after each statement. As Dag Hammarskjold noted about someone he knew: "Not knowing the question, it was easy for him to give the answer."

Remember that Zophar is addressing a man who, as it were, has just gone through bankruptcy, lost his job, had all his children killed in a head-on collision, and is himself suffering from ulcers and shingles. Yet Zophar is disturbed by Job's outburst of bitter anger. Zophar feels it isn't proper for a human to talk to God the way Job is. At the same time, he doesn't really know how to handle Job, so he bursts out with, "God is punishing you less than you deserve" (11:6). Zophar's words hang like icicles in the winter air.

Small wonder that Job retorts as he does: "You have no troubles, and yet you make fun of me; you hit a man who is about to fall" (12:5). And later, "If you were in my

119

place and I in yours, I could say everything you are saying. I could shake my head wisely and drown you with a flood of words" (16:4).

When hurting people explode in anger and speak abusively of God, we should let them do so without jumping in with words of judgment, without telling them they shouldn't feel this way or say these terrible things.

"In trouble like this I need loyal friends—whether I've forsaken God or not," Job complains (6:14).

Loyal friends would reaffirm him. They would say quietly, "I think you're working hard to find your way through, Job." "It's all right to doubt." "I'm glad you feel free to ask questions." "I can understand why you feel angry."

To be a loyal friend to someone who is questioning and maligning God is tricky. It calls for self-understanding, humility, patience, and above all, lots of love. It requires willingness to spend time listening without judging.

Have you ever accepted the challenge of becoming such a friend? Or do you withdraw from those who suffer?

We think God is destroying us when He is tuning us.

— Henry Ward Beecher

When God appears to be angry or to do us an unkindness, it is we who are altered.

— Johannes Eckhart

Is God Mad at Me?

God's anger is constant (9:13).

As Job responds to Bildad's accusations, he unleashes his anger against God. We see that his concept of God becomes more and more distorted.

He already has accused God of using him for target practice and shooting arrows at him—and not only arrows, but poisoned arrows, arrows that can kill (6:4). He has protested that he feels as if he is constantly being watched because God views him as malicious, intent on destroying others (7:12). In 7:17-19 he has called God an inspector, and in 7:20 a jailer. In 9:15 he labels God a judge.

A present-day illustration could be a traffic officer who, mounted on his motorcycle, parks around corners, waiting for Job every time he backs out of his driveway and starts down the street. Morning after morning, Job sees the policeman in his rear-view mirror. He tries to shake him, but he can't. Then a red flashing light reflects in his mirror, and a voice tells him to pull over. He protests he has done nothing wrong. The officer continues to write out a citation. Job is ordered to appear in court.

"Why do you track down all my sins and hunt down every fault I have?" Job yells at the officer as he roars away on his motorcycle (10:6).

"You know that I am not guilty," Job whimpers as he rolls up his car window and drives away. "[But you know] that no one can save me from you" (10:7).

Job arrives at court with a dry mouth and perspiring hands, and pleads for a lawyer (9:33; 16:21). He is given none. Moreover, he discovers the traffic officer has lined up witnesses against him (10:17). And then, like a bad dream, he sees the traffic officer disappear through a door in front, and then re-emerge clad in the black robes of a judge (9:15). Job realizes that the one who has filed charges against him will now judge the case. He hasn't a chance.

"I am innocent and faithful, but my words sound guilty," he complains. "Everything I say seems to condemn me.

"How can I find words to answer God?" he complains. "Though I am innocent, all I can do is beg for mercy from God my judge. Yet even then, if he lets me speak, I can't believe he would listen to me" (9:14-16).

Job's conception of God grows even more distorted. He begins to regard God as sadistic. Now he envisions Him as the patrol officer, dragging him out to the shooting field and setting him up as a target for practice.

"You jailer," he sputters angrily, as the bullets whiz around him. "Why use me for your target practice?" (7:20).

Later, in the third dialogue, Job returns to this metaphor. He envisions God dancing fiendishly around him, shooting at him from every side.

"God uses me for target practice and shoots arrows at me from every side—arrows that pierce and wound me . . ." he complains. "He wounds me again and again; he attacks like a soldier gone mad with hate" (16:12-14).

He accuses God of being so hardened He is past feeling.

"He shows no pity," Job wails (16:13). In fact, "when an innocent man suddenly dies, God laughs" (9:23).

Job is not through with his bitter, scathing attack on God. He pictures God calling in others to torment him. He believes God is no longer satisfied with just an hour of target practice. He calls his soldiers to surround Job, to dig in, and to prepare to stay to the finish.

"God is angry and rages against me," Job fumes. "He treats me like his worst enemy. He sends his army to attack me; they dig trenches and lay siege to my tent" (19:11, 12).

We stand appalled and aghast at Job's audacity in flinging these accusations in God's face. The full force of the accusations may be lost as we read the text, because the entire description is not poured out in one continuous, explosive, uninterrupted ejaculation. The picture undoubtedly is clear and complete in Job's mind. He has mulled it over and seethed inwardly as he has brooded about it. But the accusations escape from his lips in broken fragments, interspersed, amazingly enough, with wistful longing and almost kindly feelings toward God.

Is it not so too with us when we are deeply hurt, frustrated, and feeling trapped? We wheel on someone we love and begin to pour out hidden resentments and ill feelings that have been simmering within us. The angry accusations pour out, one by one, often each one more bitter and bolder that the previous one. Yet at the same time we really love the one we are attacking, and our explosions may be interspersed with comparatively good days and expressions of love and tenderness. Perhaps it is the discovery that the loved one is not casting us off that gives us the courage finally to bring to light the worst feelings we have, until all the venom has been spewed out.

The poison must be drained from our hearts. Job is draining it by directly attacking God. He is not doubting

God's existence; rather, he is beginning to believe dreadful things about Him, to suspect he has been fooled and betrayed, that God is not the God he had thought Him to be.

Job does not recognize that his present concept of God is the mistaken one. The correct one will come, but Job is not ready for the revelation that will make this clear to him. All of Job's anger and bitterness has not yet been drained away. He is still resentful and angry, still rebelling and fighting.

In grief nothing "stays put." One keeps emerging from a phase, but it always recurs. Round and round . . .
Am I going in circles or dare I hope I'm on a spiral?

— C. S. Lewis

Whom Are You Kidding, Zophar?

Then all your troubles will fade from your memory (11:16).

Whom are you kidding, Zophar? Are you so inexperienced in suffering that you do not know that the loss of a loved one leaves us forever changed? That the memory lingers on? That the pain, though dulled and bearable, is still there, and sometimes surprises us?

Twenty-two and 23 years after we had laid two infant sons to rest in tiny graves in Canada, we returned to visit those graves on a summer Sunday evening. As we drove through the tall, black, wrought-iron gates of the cemetery, the sun was bidding goodbye to the trees. Suddenly, unexpectedly, from deep within me a fountain broke through the thin crust that had covered it, and I began to weep. During the many years since the death of our first two little sons, four bright, healthy, happy youngsters had gladdened our hearts and home. Life had been very good to us. I had thought I had worked through my grief. I had thought the

125

hurts were healed. But suddenly, I was hurting all over again.

Let us be slow in making extravagant promises to our grieving, suffering friends. The pain will become more bearable as time moves on. The loneliness won't be quite as great. The depression will fade away. There will be days of happiness and thanksgiving. New love ties will be formed; new purposes for living discovered. But will we ever forget the loved person? Never! Zophar betrays his inexperience by his impossible promise.

We should so fear and love God that we do not belie, betray, slander, nor raise injurious reports against our neighbors, but apologize for them, speak well of them, and put the most charitable construction on all their actions.

— Martin Luther

Detectives and spies do not represent the Christian way of life and liberty.

— Oscar Blackwelder

The Poison of Vague Insinuations

God knows which men are worthless; he sees all their evil deeds (11:11).

Over and over, Job's friends make insinuating remarks designed to cause him to doubt his position and accept their point of view. Zophar now insinuates that in God's sight, Job is worthless and evil. In these remarks he mixes truth and falsehood.

To raise doubt by insinuating remarks is a technique the evil one has employed since the Garden of Eden.

"Did God really tell you not to eat fruit from any tree in the garden?" the snake (Satan) asked the woman (Gen. 3:1).

The insinuation was, "Did God create all these attractive trees with luscious, juicy, mouth-watering orange, yellow, red, and peach-colored fruit, hanging here ripe and accessible and then place you in the midst with a growling hungry tummy and arms long enough to reach the fruit and forbid you to eat any of it? What an unreasonable, unjust, unloving, unfeeling, sadistic Being God must be!"

Actually, God had not marked every tree forbidden, but only one.

Satan's next approach to Eve was a blatant, bold denial that what God had said would actually come true. Satan accused God of being jealous and selfish and of not wanting humans to be like Him.

Satan's insinuations about God to Eve were designed to make her doubt His word and character. Job's friends made insinuating remarks to cause Job to question his relationship with God and to force him to confess that he really hadn't been walking uprightly (even though he had). They insisted that the very fact that he was in trouble was undeniable proof of his guilt.

A senior pastor who had been idolized by his congregation finally decided he needed help, and an assistant pastor was called. The senior pastor was a gifted preacher and Bible teacher, and he began to accept invitations to preach and teach outside his home church. The younger pastor faithfully tended the flock, calling on people, organizing small support groups within the church, and visiting those in crisis situations. Being of a warm and demonstrative nature, he frequently expressed his affection for the people with hugs and embraces. The congregation loved him and were vocal in their appreciation of his ministry.

Little seeds of jealousy began to sprout and grow in the heart of the senior pastor. Slowly, vague insinuations about the moral behavior of the younger pastor began to circulate among the congregation. He denied them. When those spreading the rumors were cornered, they declared they had been misunderstood, that they really hadn't said these things. But as the rumors persisted and these people were challenged again, they began to say mysteriously that they could not tell what they knew.

Weeks and months passed, and the rumors grew more mysterious and threatening, but they were always so vague that they could not be faced and answered by the younger man. Finally, the situation became so uncomfortable and so difficult to deal with that, in spite of the congregation's overwhelming indication of their support, the assistant pastor resigned and left the parish.

Controlling people and getting one's way by making vague insinuations about the character of another is one of Satan's oldest tricks. Sorrowfully, we must admit that even God's people do this today. We need to be aware of this technique and resist it regularly.

They have healed the wound of my people lightly,
saying, "Peace, peace," when there is no peace.
— Jeremiah 6:14, RSV

Who Needs an Incorrigible Optimist?

Your life will be brighter than sunshine at noon,
and life's darkest hours will shine like the dawn
(11:17).

Viktor E. Frankl, writing of his grim year at Auschwitz and
other Nazi prisons, remarked: "The incorrigible optimists
were the most irritating companions."

Job's friends tried to cheer him up by promising him
all sorts of fantastic rewards if only he would repent and
turn to God. Zophar assured Job his future life would be
secure and full of hope.

"God will protect you and give you rest. You won't be
afraid of your enemies; many people will ask you for help,"
he declared (11:18, 19).

I suspect that the bright words of Job's friends probably
irritated him more than the scratchy burlap he wore or his
oozing, itching sores. Job cries out that his friends do not
understand and says they are drowning him with a flood of
words (16:4).

The last thing suffering people want to be told is to
cheer up. To insist they think positively in the midst of their
pain is to demand that they leap over some necessary stages

of suffering. It is like forcing orange blossoms to become sweet, juicy, refreshing oranges overnight. It causes more pain, not less, for it is like the pain a mother experiences when her baby is born prematurely. For premature births, while easier for the mother because the baby is smaller, often are more painful because the muscles have not become resilient, a process the body seems to set in motion naturally in preparation for the stretching required for birth. To tell one plunged in grief to cheer up is like demanding taut muscles to stretch before they have become soft and pliable.

"Even though I walk through the valley of the shadow of death," David wrote, "I fear no evil" (Ps. 23:4, RSV). Of course, we all would prefer leaping across the valley or running through it at top speed. But we cannot hurry grief. Grief takes time. How long depends on a person's previous track record in recovering from loss, the closeness and dependency on the one lost, and the ability to establish new relationships and to adapt. There are many variables.

In Africa, after three months people used to inquire of mourners if the bitterness of the loss was losing some of its sting. "Has it cooled off yet?" they would ask.

And in America, many say that after a year things go better. But one researcher revealed that after two years only 10 widows out of 72 said they were free of grief. Grieving is work—work that takes time. And when the grieving ones are suffering, to have to listen to the optimists' words of massive cheer is chilling and depressing indeed.

When you are suffering, take your encouragement from the faithful realists, not from the ignorant optimists. And as you minister to the grief-stricken, remember to be realistic in your counsel and care.

131

Our reaction to others depends to a large extent
on how we perceive and judge them.
— Charlotte L. Doyle

Does God Really Care About Me?

God has wisdom and power. . . . God is strong
and always victorious (12:13, 16).

Both Job and his friends spoke often of the transcendence
of God, but they viewed His super-eminence and His sovereignty from different perspectives.

"We cannot understand the great things He [God]
does," Eliphaz says (5:9), implying, "So why try?"

"God is powerful; all must stand in awe of him," Bildad
reminds Job, and adds, "Then what about man, that worm,
that insect? What is man worth in God's eyes?" (25:1, 6).

The transcendence of God caused Job's friends to worship, but at a distance with fear and trembling, afraid to
explore God's character.

Job also is aware of God's power. Perhaps because he
feels trapped, he views God as domineering and accuses
Him of using His might to control and manipulate people.

"How can a man win his case against God?" Job asks.
"How can any one argue with him? . . . God is so wise and
powerful; no man can stand up against him. . . . He takes
what he wants, and no one can stop him; no one dares ask
him, 'What are you doing?' " (9:1-4, 12).

132

Feeling cornered by God, Job laughs bitterly and complains, "Should I try force? Try force on God? Should I take him to court? Who would make him go?" (9:19).

Job shrinks under God's power. "You overpower a man," he complains (14:20). He feels trapped, like a fish caught in a bear's paw, like a chicken caught on a busy freeway with cars whizzing by.

David viewed God's transcendence in another way in Psalm 8. When he considered God's strength and power as portrayed in the created universe, controlled and directed by Him even now, he burst forth in worship and praise that the God of the universe should think and care about mere humans.

"When I look at thy heavens, the work of thy fingers, the moon and the stars which thou hast established; what is man that thou art mindful of him, and the son of man that thou dost care for him? (Ps. 8:3, 4 RSV).

A hymn writer, picking up that theme, noted with awe and wonder that he who has "the whole world in his hands," who keeps the planets of the universe spinning in orbit, also has "the tiny little baby" and you and me, too, "in his hands."

How do you view God's transcendence? Does His sovereignty strike fear into your heart, or does it provoke awe, wonder, and trust?

> Telling God frankly what I have to say to him, and listening to what he has quite personally to say to me—this is the dialogue which makes me a person, a free and responsible being It means being in fellowship with God, and that is faith.
>
> — Paul Tournier

I'm Going Straight to God About This

> But my dispute is with God, not you; I want to argue my case with him (13:3).

Chapter 13 marks a turning point in Job's relationship with his friends. From here on, the distance between them widens. Their insinuations and accusations have been so venomous, their lack of understanding so apparent, and their trite answers so unrelated to his problem that Job despairs of ever receiving help from them. He decides to go directly to God instead.

Chapter 13 is a fascinating study in how Job works up courage to approach God directly. His circuitous approach is comparable to the long preparation some baseball pitchers go through before each pitch.

Notice Job's procedure.

First he states his intention: "I want to argue my case with him [God]" (13:3).

Then he addresses his friends, "Be quiet and give me a chance to speak"—and then in a rush of bravado he adds,

134

"and let the results be what they will. I am ready to risk my life. I've lost all hope, so what if God kills me?" (13:13-15). Job apparently is trying to cover up his uneasy feeling as he contemplates what he has said he will do. As though to bolster his courage, he repeats his declaration. "I am going to state my case to him" (13:15).

He pauses, reflects, and then says hopefully that maybe God will admire his courage and treat him favorably.

He calls his friends to attention again. "Now listen to my words of explanation. I am ready to state my case" (13:17, 18).

As he draws nearer, he decides to "feel God out."

"Are you coming to accuse me, God?" he asks, and adds, "If you do, I am ready to be silent and die" (13:19).

"Speak first, O God, and I will answer," he says politely, giving God first chance (13:22).

There is no answer, so he goes on.

"Or let me speak, and you answer me" (13:22).

I envision a breathless pause at this point. Then he blurts out: "What are my sins? What wrongs have I done? What crimes am I charged with?" (13:23).

He has stated it! It is out! He waits. Silence. He waits. Still no answer.

"Why do you avoid me?" he asks God petulantly (13:24).

But God does not speak. Is God silent because Job's next words show he is not ready to listen to what God will say?

"Why do you treat me like an enemy?" Job complains, and the question lets loose once again a rushing torrent of bitter talk (13:24).

Job is still angry. God will wait to speak to His rebellious child. Job's anger has destroyed his capacity to receive. Even God won't give until we are ready to receive.

Despair is demoralizing; Hope is inspiring. Doubt is debilitating; Hope is energizing.

— W. T. McElveen

The Smooth Shall Bloom from the Rough

You destroy man's hope for life (14:19).

Job is plunged into despair again.

"You destroy man's hope for life," he complains.

Job is like a strong swimmer caught too far out to sea for his own safety. Exhausted and chilled through, he gives up hope of reaching the lights on shore. He rolls over on his back and floats, well aware that huge waves may submerge him or sharks may discover him. Momentarily, he doesn't care. He is too weary.

Then the flicking of a shark's tail arouses him. He rolls over and begins to swim again, aware of new energy infusing his tired body. Maybe, he thinks as he escapes from the shark, maybe he will reach shore after all.

So it continues. There will be ups and downs. Good days. Bad days. Very bad days. Days when one's faith and hope seem strong. Days when one feels dead and unable to believe.

"Even Luther said, 'Sometimes I believe and sometimes I doubt,' didn't he?" Bob Lange said to me one day when I was visiting him. He sighed and said, "It will be a profound relief to die. Sometimes it takes so much effort to

136

believe." He paused, "I think I understand better now the meaning of the phrase, 'the fight of faith.' Sometimes it is a fight to continue to believe."

Mercifully, viewed against an entire life span, those times of severe testing are relatively few and short-lived, but if and when they come, they bring anguish.

The road to recovery from loss is never a steady uphill drive. Rather, the road dips and bends and then ascends again. But always, hope is like the twinkling lights on the shore, coaxing one on.

> To go on forever and fail and go on again,
> And be mauled to the earth, and arise,
> And content for the shade of a word,
>   and a thing not seen with the eyes,
> With the half of a broken hope for a pillow at night,
> That somehow the right is right,
> And the smooth shall bloom from the rough.
>
> — Robert Louis Stevenson

"The hope placed before us . . . [is] an anchor for our lives. It is safe and sure" (Heb. 6:18, 19).

A friendly face masking a cold heart . . .

— John Baillie

Scare Tactics

A wicked man who oppresses others will be in
torment as long as he lives (15:20).

As Job's friends begin the second round of dialogue with
him, they realize that scolding and admonishing has gotten
them nowhere. Job can't be scolded into repentance. So
they try scare tactics. Eliphaz sketches a grim picture of what
Job can expect if he doesn't repent.

> Voices of terror will scream in his ears, and robbers
> attack when he thinks he is safe. He has no hope of
> escaping from darkness, for somewhere a sword is wait-
> ing to kill him, and vultures are waiting to eat his corpse.
> He knows his future is dark; disaster, like a powerful
> king, is waiting to attack him (15:21-24).

Bildad picks up the theme and adds some choice bits
of his own. He declares that Job will be caught in a trap
from which he cannot escape. (Job already feels this way!)
Bildad refers to the disease that has spread over Job's body,
classifying it as deadly, declaring Job's arms and legs will
rot and fall away and that he will be dragged off to face
King Death (18:13, 14).

"From east to west, all who hear of his fate shudder
and tremble with fear. That," declares Bildad triumphantly,

138

wagging his finger, "is the fate of evil men, the fate of those who care nothing for God" (18:20, 21).

His last statement is extraordinary. If Job cared nothing for God, would he be struggling to understand Him? Would he be engaged in a lover's quarrel?

Zophar, in addition to pointing out Job's sins, also emphasizes the fact that Job will be blown away like dust and will vanish like a dream. He does not stop with this but goes on with more gory details.

> God will punish him in fury and anger. When he tries to escape from an iron sword, a bronze bow will shoot him down. An arrow sticks through his body; its shiny point drips with his blood, and terror grips his heart (20:23-25).

Even today, some who call themselves God's people resort to scare tactics. When they cannot get those "under their authority" to "obey God," (in other words, to obey them), they threaten and anathematize them.

Job's friends presumed to be the voice of God for Job. Eliphaz said, "God offers you comfort; why still reject it? We have spoken for him" (15:11). To their way of thinking, for Job to reject their words was for him to reject God. Thus they felt justified in uttering threats.

But Job was not to be moved by intimidation. The threatening words of his friends only reinforced his declarations that he was not guilty as they claimed he was.

The good shepherd, Jesus said, leads his sheep, and the sheep follow him. He doesn't drive. There is a vast difference. Satan cracks the whip, but our Shepherd calls by name.

Insecurities are enemies of open communication
and true community.

— Gerhard E. Frost

Who Can Shout the Loudest?

We learned our wisdom from gray-haired men—
men born before your father (15:10).

The conversation between Job and his friends has degen-
erated into childish competition. "I know lots more than
you," Eliphaz says, in effect. "When your dad was running
around in diapers, my gray-haired, wise old father was already teaching me."

Competition often grows out of a feeling of insecurity
and inferiority—and of having to prove ourselves. The person who does not doubt his self-worth likewise does not
feel the need to toot his own horn.

The props have been knocked out from under Job *and*
his friends. They haven't been able to come up with con-
clusive answers, so they resort to shouting a little louder,
making more extravagant claims for themselves and more
pointed accusations. As is often said, more heat is being
generated than light.

When hurting, perplexed people come to us for counsel, we too often feel inadequate. There are alternatives,
however, to preaching at them. Prayerfully, we can ask God
to bring to our attention others better able to offer the

needed counsel. To direct a seeking one to a person who can help him lets him know that we accept his hurt as real, that we care and want to help. The gospels relate the accounts of a number of thwarted, frustrated people who brought their suffering friends to One who could help, the Lord Jesus. Does Eliphaz have no one to whom he could direct Job? Is this why he is shouting now?

Some confessed that they had wept, like the comrade who answered my question of how he had gotten over his edema, by confessing, "I have wept it out of my system."

— Viktor Frankl (commenting on his years in the concentration camp)

Crying

I have cried until my face is red, and my eyes are swollen and circled with shadows (16:16).

Job, a man, was speaking. The culture and customs of his day let a man cry. Crying was not considered weakness. It was an acceptable expression of suffering.

For almost nine years, our family lived on the lower slopes of Mount Kilimanjaro in East Africa. There men also cried when sorrow visted their homes. In the rural areas where we lived, men who had experienced bereavement were not expected to return to their work for at least a week. During this time, friends and relatives came to the house to sit and listen and talk about the one who had just died, to cry together and wipe tears and drink tea.

Our culture has denied men the freedom to cry. The result is that after years of pushing down and denying their emotions, some men are so out of touch with their feelings they do not know how they feel any more. How tragic! Tears are not signs of weakness, but rather of the courage to suffer.

But women in America are also misunderstood when they cry. Women are allowed to cry, but only because they are considered weak and emotional and incapable of controlling their feelings. "Strong" women do not cry.

I was speaking once at a public meeting on the poverty in today's world. I explained that some countries are so poor and are experiencing so much internal strife and confusion that nations that could offer hope tend to classify them as hopeless. The reasoning of the prosperous nations is that they have only limited economic aid to offer, and so they must give it to those countries that show promise of economic stability and of a decreasing need for aid. The other nations, sometimes referred to as fourth-world countries, need much more help than is available. And so there is no other alternative, perhaps, than to write them off as hopeless.

As I spoke of this situation, I surprised myself by becoming so overcome with tears that I could not go on, and I had to sit down. A well-meaning friend patted me on my knee and whispered, "It's because you're so tired."

Her comment produced a mixed reaction in my heart, and the tears overflowed again. My schedule had been very heavy, and I was tired. At the same time, the tension of trying to reconcile our American affluence with survival needs of fourth-world countries had been building up within me, and I needed the release tears brought. Maybe, I thought later, it was good that I cried. Maybe the Lord could use tears more than words. Sometimes mustering stoic control can have the opposite effect from what we hope to achieve.

In Africa, when our little children (only six, seven, eight, and nine years old) would leave to go by bus to boarding school 300 miles away, I would smile brightly, joke, and wave until their bus had turned the corner and was out of sight. I reasoned that I had to be brave and "bear up" and "not break down" for their sakes, even though I felt as if my innards were being ground up.

Then the day came for our family to leave Tanzania and return to the States. A number of our African friends had taken the bus or walked to the tiny airport to bid us farewell. At the terminal, they put our family in the center, stood in a circle around us, and sang and prayed. The pilot of our plane, standing on the sidelines, watched with interest.

Airborne, our pilot directed our plane so we flew over the pass between Kibo and Mawenzi, the two peaks of Mount Kilimanjaro. Then, unexpectedly, he dipped the wings as though in farewell for us. During our years on the lower slopes of Mount Kilimanjaro, I had learned to love the mountain and the people of the mountain who had opened their hearts to include our family. Suddenly I began to cry. Our eight-year-old daughter, who was sitting some seats ahead of me, heard me and came back to me. Standing in the aisle, she put her hands on her hips and surveyed me.

"Serves you right," she said, unexpectedly.

Stunned, I stopped crying.

"What?" I stammered.

"Serves you right," she repeated. "Now you know how your little kids felt when you sent them off to boarding school."

What I had thought to be courageous support, she had interpreted as a lack of love and caring.

The more we can allow people to express themselves in ways that are natural for them, the easier we make it for them to recover from loss. But there does come the time, even when sorrow has been immense, when we have to stop crying. Job will have to dry his eyes, too. But not quite yet.

144

For there is one God, and there is one mediator between God and men, the man Christ Jesus, who gave himself as a ransom for all.

— 1 Tim. 2:5,6 RSV

Who'll Take My Side?

I want someone to plead with God for me, as a man pleads for his friend. There is someone in heaven to stand up for me and take my side (16:21, 19).

Some scholars believe the Book of Job is one of the earliest biblical accounts, actually preceding the time of the prophets who foretold the coming of the Savior. If this is indeed so, we marvel at Job's sensing the need of a mediator.

We find the first indication of this need when we see that he offered sacrifices for each of his children in order to purify them. Now, when he feels God is angry with him, he feels the need of a mediator to intercede on his behalf.

"There is no one to step between us," he cries out, "no one to judge both God and me" (9:33).

He seems to grasp, too, that the mediator must be someone in heaven who will plead his case for him. For Job, although he has declared his innocence of specific sins, has not denied his sinful state. Let's try to understand the difference.

145

Up until this time Job steadfastly has resisted the pressure of his friends to confess some sin he has not committed. He asserts over and over that, to his knowledge, he is not guilty of any particular sin terrible enough to have caused him the suffering he is experiencing.

But while he asserts and declares his innocence of a particular known sin, Job does not deny his sinful state and nature. Several times he refers to the fact that he is a sinner, guilty of sins that no soap can wash away (7:21; 9:28, 29; 14:4). Further he states—although he doesn't use those exact words—that it is God's responsibility to forgive sin.

Job never denied that he was a sinner, and without question he recognized the need of a mediator between God and himself. How happy Job would have been if he could have been in that place of history where we are, if he could have known that indeed "There is one God, and there is one mediator between God and men, the man Christ Jesus" (1 Tim. 2:5, RSV).

But this comforting assurance, which may be ours, is not granted to Job. We have been assured that we have a Mediator who not only reconciles us to God, but who stands now before God, pleading for us. But Job's hope cannot rest in a historical fact, for the death and resurrection of the Mediator, Christ Jesus, has not yet taken place. Nor can his hope rest in the accounts that prophesy this intervention of God on our behalf. Yet instinctively, his heart reaches out in expectation. There must be someone, he says, groping, who will intercede for him, someone who will save him.

No persons should judge unless they ask themselves in absolute honesty whether in a similar situation they might not have done the same.

— Viktor Frankl

You Shouldn't Get So Angry

Job, can't people like you ever be quiet? . . . You are only hurting yourself with your anger (18:1, 4).

Job's anger was burning white hot, and he was letting it erupt like a hot springs geyser in Yellowstone. But when he did, he found that it separated him from his friends. Uncomfortable and appalled, they drew back, skaking their heads. He shouldn't talk like that, they said.

Expressed anger does tend to separate. Few can listen to it objectively and quietly. Consequently the angry one, sensing the threat of rejection, frequently bottles up his or her anger. Shut up inside, it heats until sooner or later it forms juices that erode the stomach or intestines, or sets afire inflammations in the joints, or sends the blood pressure soaring.

To listen quietly, wisely, and with understanding to an angry person is not easily learned. But if accepting, nonjudgmental listening can be offered, we present a gift of priceless therapeutic value to the bewildered, suffering one.

147

Magdalene Lange tells of her struggle during the three years her husband, Bob, was slowly dying.

"Each new deterioration angered me," Magdalene confesses. "Bob walked into the house one day with his mouth set in a firm, hard line. He threw a stick on the floor and fell heavily into the big white arm chair in our living room. And then I saw that the stick on the floor was a cane. Suddenly I found myself running up the stairs to our bedroom. I wanted to scream, to break windows, to yell at God, to swear, to curse. I stood facing the painted wall of our bedroom and suddenly found myself pounding it with my fists. Hot tears coursed down my cheeks. And then I felt, from behind, arms around me. Bob buried his head in the hollow of my shoulder.

" 'Oh, Babe,' he was whispering.

"I felt the anger draining out of me. Turning, I put my arms around him.

" 'Never mind,' I said, 'I just needed . . . a swearing wall, some cold unfeeling lath and plaster on which to vent my anger.' "

There were many, many other days when Magdalene felt the need to vent her feelings. But Bob's quiet acceptance of her stormy attacks against God enabled her to get her anger out. When Bob's death finally came, no residue of anger was left. In its place were the gratitude, acceptance, and trust that had taken over. This was apparent to others also.

"After the funeral," Magdalene said, "I noticed our yard needed attention. I wondered why the gardener we had hired during Bob's illness hadn't come. I was just beginning to think I would have to look for another when he showed up.

"At the end of the day he rang the doorbell and said his work was finished and he was going. He almost filled the door frame as he stood there, young, straight-backed, and bronzed with our California sun. He picked thoughtfully

148

at a callous on his right palm. I sensed he had more he wanted to say.

" 'Yes?' I encouraged him.

"He stopped picking at his callous and looked at me.

" 'I'm sorry I delayed coming back,' he began. 'I heard what happened. Usually when I go to a place where some-one has died, it's so gloomy and depressing I can hardly stand it. But here today it was—so different. There seemed to be peace around.' He quickly brushed back his hair from his eyes. 'And sort of a quiet happiness. It was a funny feeling—I felt really good, you know.' "

Job's anger made his friends nervous. They scolded him for it. When he persisted in openly venting it, they shut him out and withdrew, plunging Job into even deeper depression.

Bob accepted Magdalene during her stormy periods of deep anger. In loving her he released her, and at last she found a place of peace and rest. We can do the same when our friends are hurting and angry.

149

If our trust is placed in human beings, we shall end in despairing of everyone. . . . Our Lord trusted no man, yet He was never suspicious, never bitter.

— Oswald Chambers

Forsaken

God has made my brothers forsake me; I am a stranger to those who knew me; my relatives and friends are gone (19:13, 14).

Outside, the wind howled and whipped the snow around in eddies. Inside, alone in the hut planted on the dark immensity of the Ross Ice Barrier near the South Pole, Richard Byrd fought for his life. Inadequate ventilation earlier had depleted his oxygen supply, weakening him. Then a faulty stove, which provided life-sustaining heat, slowly began to emit carbon monoxide fumes that threatened to kill him. Byrd wrote in his book *Alone*:

Death now was a stranger sitting in a darkened room, secure in the knowledge that he would be there when I was gone. Deep waves of fear, a fear I had never known before, swept through me and settled deep within . . . I realized then that only two things really matter to a man, regardless of who he is; and they are *the affection and understanding of his family*. Anything and everything else he creates are insubstantial; they are ships given over to the mercy of the winds and tides of prejudice [italics mine].

150

Many a prisoner of war in Vietnam and Laos kept hope alive only by reminding himself that a wife or family was waiting for him at home. But when they returned, many found no wives. They had divorced them and remarried. These men, who had thought they had suffered as much as they possibly could bear, discovered there was more suffering to bear.

Job is making that discovery now.

> Those who were guests in my house have forgotten me; my servant girls treat me like a stranger and a foreigner. When I call a servant, he doesn't answer— even when I beg him to help me. . . . My own brothers won't come near me (19:15-17).

Should this bitter experience be ours, we can remember that we have a God who has been tempted in every way we have. Our Savior knew what it was to have His disciples forsake Him and flee, misunderstanding Him and leaving Him alone. Even more awful, His Father abandoned Him and let Him suffer to the point of death. It is the One who has experienced being forsaken in this way who stands ready to help and save us.

When I no more can stir my soul to move,
And life is but the ashes of a fire;
When I can but remember that my
heart once used to live and love,
      long and aspire—
Oh, be thou then the first, the one thou art;
Be thou the calling, before all answering love,
and in me wake hope, fear, boundless desire.

                                   — George MacDonald

The Cry of a Breaking Man

God has blocked the way, and I can't get through;
he has hidden my path in darkness (19:8).

Chapter 19 records the cry of a man who is breaking. Note the myriad of emotions expressed.

Job feels misunderstood. "Why do you keep tormenting me with words?" he asks his friends. "Time after time you insult me. . . . You regard my troubles as proof of my guilt" (19:1-3, 5).

Job feels abandoned and lonely. "No one is listening; no one hears my cry," he exclaims (19:7).

Job feels frustrated and hemmed in. "God has blocked the way, and I can't get through," he complains (19:8). His back is against the wall.

He is still staggering under the heavy financial losses he has sustained. "He has taken away all my wealth," he complains (19:9).

His self-esteem is wounded; he feels his reputation has been destroyed. "[God has] destroyed my reputation" (19:9).

All hope is gone. "He uproots my hope" (19:10).

Job is convinced God is angry with him. "God . . . rages against me; he treats me like his worst enemy" (19:11).

Even Job's body has become repulsive to him. He describes his skin as darkening and peeling (30:30), with oozing sores (7:5). His face is gaunt and haggard, his eyes are sunken deep, his arms and legs are like toothpicks (19:20). Fits of depression (7:16, 30:15) cause him to weep helplessly (16:16). Insomnia has etched purple shadows around his bloodshot eyes (7:4). He squints, for even his vision is failing (16:16). His vile breath drives away his wife (19:17).

And worst of all, he sees no end, no way out (19:12). He believes his troubles are with him to stay.

Psychologists stress how important it is that hurting people know there is someone who cares. Job catches a glimmer of this in 19:25, 27: "But I know there is someone in heaven who will come at last to my defense. I will see him with my own eyes, and he will not be a stranger."

Only this hope keeps Job from breaking completely.

Never look for justice in this world, but never cease to give it.

— Oswald Chambers

Why Does the Bad Guy Prosper?

> Why does God let evil men . . . grow old and prosper? (21:7).

Why does the bad guy succeed and the good guy fail? How many times have you asked yourself that question—especially after being conned or lied about by a deceiver.

Job further declares:

> [The wicked] have children and grand children, and live to watch them all grow up. God does not bring disaster on their homes; they never have to live in terror. Yes, all their cattle breed and give birth without trouble. Their children run and play like lambs and dance to the music of harps and flutes. They live out their lives in peace and quietly die without suffering (21:8-13).

The question is all the more perplexing for Job because, as he observes, the wicked live without God and tell God to leave them alone because they can manage on their own. "They don't want to know his will for their lives," Job complains. "They think there is no need to serve God nor any advantage in praying to him. They claim they succeed by their own strength" (21:14-16).

The psalmist also struggled with this problem.

> I had nearly lost confidence, my faith was almost gone because I was jealous of the proud when I saw that things go well for the wicked. . . . I tried to think this problem through, but it was too difficult for me until I went into your Temple. Then I understood what will happen to the wicked. . . . When my thoughts were bitter and my feelings were hurt, I was as stupid as an animal; I did not understand you. . . . What else do I have in heaven but you? Since I have you, what else could I want on earth? My mind and body may grow weak, but God is my strength; he is all I ever need (Ps. 73:2-26).

Job may not find any more answers to his questions about evil than you will. But like the psalmist, he will find strength to carry on in everyday living as he visits the temple, as he meets his God.

But Job is not ready for this yet. His thoughts are still bitter. His feelings are hurt, and he does not consider himself stupid and in need of instruction. He is still arguing. He has not come to the end of himself. Perhaps that is what makes the question such a major issue.

If I cannot find Thee, O God, let me search my
heart and know whether it is not rather I who am
blind than you who are obscure, and I who am
fleeing from you rather than you from me.

— John Baillie

Hey, God! Don't You Hear Me?

Why doesn't God set a time for judging, a day of
justice for those who serve him? (24:1).

Job has called God his enemy. Now he accuses God of
ignoring him. Being ignored is sometimes more difficult to
handle than being attacked. To be ignored hits hard at self-
esteem. One can rebut an attack, but when one is ignored,
there is no one to talk to. Being ignored creates a feeling
of frustrated helplessness and worthlessness.

"How long is all this injustice going to continue, Lord?"
Job asks, knocking at God's door. But the doorbell doesn't
work, and pounding brings no response.

A friend of mine was called to a new venture: the opening of a church in an office building in downtown Chicago.
The news media publicized the venture, bringing public attention to focus on it. My friend felt the pressure to succeed.

"But I faced even a greater struggle," he admitted.
"Fellow pastors, who did not approve of the project,
avoided me at meetings, or if they talked to me, they talked
only about other subjects. Being ignored, I discovered, was

even more difficult to handle than being criticized. I became more and more frustrated. The work also proved to be far more difficult than I had guessed. My frustration at last settled like a billiard ball in my back. The doctor diagnosed it as arthritis."

My friend's doctor advised moving to a less demanding job, but my friend felt he could not because he believed God had called him to that place.

Job's frustration has resulted because he has believed he is right, but he cannot understand why God seems to be ignoring him. And not only is he frustrated, but he is growing bitter too.

"When men have learned not to be frustrated because their wishes are not immediately fulfilled and not to be bitter because the world has proved tougher and more complex than they had dreamed, then they may be in a mood to value truth very highly," Gunnar Myrdal observes in Asian Drama.

Frustration and bitterness have not yet been drained out of Job's heart. There is not sufficient room yet for revelation and understanding.

Nothing less than presence—loving, speaking, revealing—nothing less than the God who offers himself as solace and salvation can suffice for Job.

— Gerhard E. Frost

Why Don't You Straighten Things Out, God?

Why doesn't God set . . . a day of justice for those who serve him? (24:1)

Job now raises the question of how there can be a just God in an unjust and immoral world. Not only does he consider his own situation, but his description of social ills in chapter 24 is eloquent.

He speaks of graft and trickery, of taking advantage of widows (today's list would include divorcées). He graphically describes the plight of the migrants and the misery of the poor and the way they are exploited. Job faces the suffering and injustices of the world and asks questions. His friends ignore these things, and quote sayings to solve any uneasiness they feel.

We do the same. Or we say, "If they weren't so lazy, they'd have something." "If they'd kill their sacred cows and eat them instead of worshiping them, they wouldn't be so hungry."

The fact that Job, rich man though he is (or was), is concerned about these ills of society is quite remarkable. Many a wealthy person has gained his wealth by exploitation of the poor. Many have little or no concern about the lot of the poor. Obsessed with the desire to reach the top, they either use everybody or push them out of the way.

Job voices real concern. He is not insensitive nor blind to the world around him, and the injustices he sees hurt him. In fact, he wonders whether this could even happen if God were really in control.

I too, at times, have had similar thoughts. But the best way I have found to handle it is to become personally involved in helping ease some of the suffering. When I do that, I don't have much time for questions—questions that very likely will never be fully answered in this life.

Intermission

Reference: Chapter 28.

The fear of the Lord is the beginning of wisdom:
and the knowledge of the holy is understanding.

— Proverbs 9:10, KJV

Intermission

Wisdom is not to be found among men (28:13).

Commentators have puzzled over the inclusion of chapter 28, the Song of Wisdom, in the Book of Job. It seems to be an intrusion or interjection. Probably this was intentional. We are ready to move into the final scenes of our drama. Job's friends have failed to help him because their theology was wrong. They believed that success always follows "right-doing" and trouble follows wrongdoing. Wrong theology leads to wrong living. Job's friends' approach has been a negative approach and attack.

New characters will not appear.

It was not uncommon for Greek plays to have a chorus sing while stage props were being changed for a new scene. Can we not then picture the curtain falling on Job and his friends after their third dialogue? A guitarist, let us say, walks out, takes his place in front of the curtain, and begins to strum his instrument and sing the Song of Wisdom. We sit back and relax.

The drama has led us through a series of heated verbal encounters. A suffering man has laid bare his hurt. Emotions and pitch of voices have climbed steadily. We, the readers or observers of the drama, need a brief rest, a time to recover before the final scene. Introducing the Song of Wisdom, a quite unrelated theme, acts as a pacing device.

The song extols wisdom. The singer begins by declaring that wisdom is not to be found in the achievement of technological skills. The writer of the song describes the mining ventures of his day, which probably were equivalent to the 20th-century achievement of sending men to the moon. But we err in thinking that technological advances will solve our moral problems, the singer suggests. If the singer were living today, he probably would ask how we can pride ourselves in flying to the moon when we cannot make the streets safe for people to walk during the day.

Science does not reveal wisdom for right living. In fact, true wisdom, the singer declares, is known only to God. He closes with: "God said to men, 'To be wise, you must have reverence for the Lord, To understand, you must turn from evil' " (28:28).

Job has been exceedingly brash and irreverent in some of the accusations he has hurled at God. Is this the "evil" he must turn from in order to understand?

Scene VII
The Garbage Dump

Job

Elihu: his friend.

Reference: 32:1—37:24

When he [the devil] lies, he speaks according to his own nature, for he is a liar and the father of lies.
— John 8:44, RSV

God is not a God of confusion but of peace.
— 1 Corinthians 14:33, RSV

Don't Add to My Confusion!

Elihu, the friend who now appears on the stage, seems to be able to summarize Job's dilemma quite well:

> Now this is what I heard you say: "I am not guilty; I have done nothing wrong. I am innocent and free from sin. But God finds excuses for attacking me and treats me like an enemy. He binds chains on my feet; he watches every move I make" (33:8-11).

But having stated this, Elihu takes off on a tirade that goes on for six chapters. In his counsel are words of wisdom and truth intermingled with falsehood.

In a class I taught, I jotted down 20 of Elihu's statements. I asked the students to mark the statements true or false. When we considered the answers, some unquestionably fell into the categories of true and false. But many were hotly debated, with students taking each side. Finally one cried out, "His statements are so confusing! They can be taken in so many different ways!"

The point had been made. Elihu is confusing in what he has to say. The Gahuku people of New Guinea would describe Job's dilemma as he listens to Elihu in this way: "His one ear was telling him one thing and the other ear was telling him something else, and he didn't know which one to believe."

Sowing seeds of confusion is one of the oldest tricks of the evil one, and don't forget the major role he is playing in this drama.

All the cults use the device of producing confusion. They begin expounding a doctrine listeners can agree with. Once they have their listeners agreeing, subtly and cannily the cultists introduce their differing points of view. The result is usually thoroughly confused people.

God is not a God of confusion. When He speaks to us, it is with clarity. As someone observed, hearing God speak is like turning up the amplifier so every word comes through distinctly and clearly. No room is left for doubt.

"If in doubt, don't," Oswald Chambers succinctly advised. Wise words. God does not speak in a confusing way or throw us into confusion. He speaks clearly and leads us in peace.

Life is fragile.
Handle it with prayer.

Struck Down in Mid-Life

> And Job again took up his discourse, and said:
> "Oh, that I were as in the months of old, as in
> the days when God watched over me; when his
> lamp shone upon my head, and by his light I
> walked through darkness; as I was in my autumn
> days, when the friendship of God was upon my
> tent" (29:1-4, RSV).

Struck down in "autumn days." Days of reaping the harvest after years of sowing. Days of seeing children blossom and mature and become loyal, interesting, enjoyable friends to their parents. Days of enjoying one's work because one can do it with the ease and confidence that years of experience bring. Days of basking in the prestige that advancement and success have brought. Days of relative confidence because one is part of the "command generation." But to lose control at this point in one's life is shattering.

Just how old Job was we are not sure. His children are described as young adults, but no mention is made of their being married. In 15:10 Eliphaz declares that the elders among them were older than Job's father. Undoubtedly, Job was in his middle years. Although he had witnessed calamity happening to others, like many of us he probably had thought it would never happen to him.

"I always expected to live a long life and to die at home in comfort," he says in 29:18.

Life is fragile. Job hadn't expected to be cut down in his middle years. He has been caught unprepared. For all of us, growing old is no excuse to afford ourselves the luxury of rebellion or unbelief. But the autumn of life is perhaps Satan's favorite time to tempt us with the need to feel sorry for ourselves. How much better instead to focus on the faithfulness of God as we have experienced it throughout our lifetimes.

> Our Lord cannot do anything for us if we think we
> are sufficient of ourselves. We have to enter into
> his kingdom through the door of destitution.
>
> — Oswald Chambers

Fantasia

Job began speaking again (29:1).

As the final scenes are introduced, Job speaks again. At the beginning, you will recall he was absorbed in giving expression to his death wish. Now he slips into fantasy. He is more romantic than realistic.

We often see this characteristic in those who are grieving. As they talk about the one who has died, we sometimes listen with amazement as a former abusive alcoholic is portrayed as an ideal husband and father.

Job, however, speaks romantically not about his dead children, but about himself. Perhaps one reason for this is that he again has been pushed against a wall. His friends repeatedly have bruised his self-esteem. To protect himself and to help build his confidence in himself, he begins to reminisce about his accomplishments in the past.

He also feels ignored—both by his friends and by God. Often when we feel ignored by others, we almost spontaneously begin to rehearse our achievements so others will hear and take note of us. Chapter 29 is Job's cry for recognition. Because his feeling of being ignored is acute, his claims are extravagant.

He begins with how it was when he was somebody—when he was pastor of the largest church in the district, we could say, or when every pew was filled—or when the organization he headed was thriving—or when he was president of the corporation or manager of the store. Listen to Job.

> Whenever the city elders met and I took my place among them, young men stepped aside as soon as they saw me, and old men stood up to show me respect. The leaders of the people would stop talking; even the most important men kept silent.
>
> Everyone who saw me or heard of me had good things to say about what I had done. . . . Men who were in deepest misery praised me, and I helped widows find security. I have always acted justly and fairly. I was eyes for the blind and feet for the lame. I was like a father to the poor and took the side of strangers in trouble. . . .
>
> Everyone was always praising me . . . .When I gave advice, people were silent and listened carefully to what I said; they had nothing to add when I had finished. . . .
>
> I smiled on them when they had lost confidence; my cheerful face encouraged them. I took charge and made the decisions; I led them as a king leads his troops (29:7-25).

Really, Job. You are too much. Is your ego so bruised? Have you become so unsure of yourself that rejection by your peers is driving you to boast? How pitiful!

When people begin to live in the land of "has-been," can we recognize their need for feeling worthy now? The teen-ager, the unemployed or underemployed, the soon-to-be-retired, the housewife, the elderly—all know the ache of feeling insignificant and worthless. One reason is because in our culture we all too often equate worth with productivity.

Interestingly enough, Job relates as many satisfying relational experiences as he does career accomplishments. Would not a re-emphasis in our teaching on the value and worth of just being a whole, genuine person meet much of the need for recognition? So then, rather than covering our ears or sighing when recitals of past accomplishments begin, how much better if we can in some way help our friends to believe they are of value just as they are—now. Then such rehearsals of past accomplishments or present feverish activities will not be necessary.

One day years ago, as I was caring for our newest baby, the truth that God loves me as I am now came home to me in a fresh way. I took my pen and wrote the following:

Baby,
> you are important to me.
> Valuable.
> Worthwhile.
> You can't do a thing yet except demand attention
>> and care from me,
> yet I love you.
Deeply.
Passionately.
I love you for yourself.
For what you are now,
> a wriggling, helpless, sometimes happy, some-
>> times cranky bundle of humanity.
Your presence fills our home with happiness.
I love you and enjoy you for what you are *now*.
Not for what you will become,
> but for what you are *now*.
And understanding that this is the way I love you
> makes it easier for me
> to understand and believe
> that this is the way God loves me now.*

---

*From *Devotions for a New Mother* by Mildred Tengbom. Copyright © 1977, 1983 by Mildred Tengbom.

If Job's friends could have helped him see the positive influences suffering can have, instead of reminding him of his losses and insinuating he was responsible for them all, Job would not have slipped into extreme fantasy.

Let the past sleep,
but let it sleep on the bosom of Christ,
and go out into the irresistible future with him.

— Oswald Chambers

For now I trust in God for strength
I trust him to employ
His love for me and change my sighs
To thankful hymns of joy.

— Nahum Tate

If Only

If only my life could once again be as it was when
God watched over me (29:2).

If only—two of the saddest and most futile words grieving
ones can utter. It is the tragedy of the "might have been."

If only we had gone to the doctor earlier. If only we
had taken out more insurance. If only I had been more
sensitive to how my child felt. If only I had taken more
interest in my child. If only I had acquainted myself with my
child's friends. If only I had kept the lines of communication
open between my wife and me. If only I had recognized the
worth of that promotion. If only I had disciplined myself to
study.

On and on the "if onlys" can go.

Beware of them. To utter them is wasted breath. To
think about them and dwell on them is wasted energy. The
past is past. Say instead: "Here I am now. I was wrong,

174

and this is the way things are. Lord, where do You want me to go from here?"

But the "if onlys" can recall happy times too. If only my husband were living now, how much fun we would have! If only I had my health back . . . If only I could play with my grandchildren again.

Cherishing happy memories is all right and even to be encouraged. Healing can come through memories relived.

But at the same time the clothes of the loved one must be given away, the closet emptied. The wheelchair must be accepted. Inactivity must find new ways of participation. We need to live in the reality of today and look to the morrow of hope and promise.

Memories, if they assume their rightful places, will not weave restraining webs around us. Rather, they will motivate us to live life to the full during the days that remain. But memories too need to come under the authority and direction of the indwelling Christ.

The worst power of an evil mood is this—
It makes the bastard self
seem in the right.

— George MacDonald

Farther into Fantasy

I swear that every word is true. Let Almighty God
answer me (31:35).

Having made fantastic declarations as to his previous accomplishments, Job now lets everyone know what a good
man he has been, how he has *never* sinned.

Again, Job's friends have forced him into this position
by their unrelenting attacks on his integrity. Whereas at the
beginning Job rightfully asserted his innocence of any particular, deliberate sin that should have caused his troubles,
now he extravagantly declares he has *never* sinned. One
by one he enumerates the sins of which his friends have
accused him, and methodically he declares his absolute innocence (the italics are mine).

"I have made a solemn promise *never* to look with lust
at a girl" (31:1).

"I swear I have *never* acted wickedly and *never* tried
to deceive others" (31:5).

"I have *never* refused to help the poor; *never* have I
let widows live in despair" (31:16).

"[I have *never*] cheated an orphan" (31:21).

"I have *never* trusted in riches or taken pride in my wealth"(31:24).

"I have *never* been glad when my enemies suffered, or pleased when they met with disaster" (31:29)

"Other men try to hide their sins, but I have *never* concealed mine" (31:33).

Chapter 31 hangs heavy with over 40 usages of "I" and 13 appearances of "never."

In Job's exaggerated denial of any guilt and in his declaration that he has never sinned (or if he has, that he is quick to confess it), we see him moving into a setting where his vision is distorted.

"We paint all our ladies' restrooms pink," a restaurant manager told me. "Pink reflects pleasingly on the skin and makes ladies believe they have healthy skin tone. When they feel healthy, they eat more."

What the ladies see in the mirror is not what they truly are.

When Job sees himself now as nearly sinless, he is not seeing what he truly is. And in choosing to see himself in this light, Job moves out of harmonious relationship with God. He moves from truth to error. Satan has not succeeded in getting Job to deny faith in the existence of God, but he has been successful in tripping Job into error about his own nature. By denying his sinfulness and shifting from being a forgiven sinner to being a self-sanctified saint, he slips from dependence on grace to dependence on fulfilling the Law.

It is time for God to come to the rescue.

My spirit hopes in God to set me free
From the low self
loathed of the higher me.

— John Baillie

Which of Me Is for Real?

Nothing clean can ever come from anything as unclean as man (14:4).

I have made a solemn promise *never* to look with lust at a girl . . . . Other men try to hide their sins, but I have *never* concealed mine. . . .I swear that *every* word is true (Job 31:1, 33, 35, italics mine).

Job, are you schizophrenic? With one breath you confess that no good thing dwells in you. Then, days later, you brag that you have never turned your head to watch a pretty girl walk down the street. You really did make both statements!

Which Is Me?

Within my earthly temple there's a crowd;
There's one of us that's humble, one that's proud.
There's one that's brokenhearted for his sins,
There's one that unrepentant sits and grins;
There's one that loves his neighbor as himself,
And one that cares for nought but fame and pelf
    [wealth].

From such corroding care I should be free
If I could once determine which is me.

— E. S. Martin

Whoever I am, Thou knowest, O Lord, I am Thine!

— Dietrich Bonhoeffer

What are you holding in your hand, Job? A mirror? For me? Why for me? I couldn't be guilty of the same thing, could I, Job? Oh, come now, Job, you're not suggesting there are really two of me inside of me?

How did you know?

Thou shalt not make God the scapegoat for thy emotional wounds and thy psychic scars. Thou shalt free thyself of the distortions which block thy way to His presence, and by that freedom thou shalt commune at last with Him, the source of truth, the giver of peace.

— Joshua Loth Liebman

Stop Blaming God

To his sins he adds rebellion; in front of us all he mocks God (34:37)

Is Elihu getting closer to Job's real problem? We have listened to Job's countless affirmations of innocence, which were justified at first but now seem to be in error. And have we ever heard him praying: "Search me, O God, and know my heart! Try me and know my thoughts! And see if there be any wicked way in me, and lead me in the way everlasting!" (Ps. 139:23, 24, RSV)?

Job's heart has been too rebellious to pray like this.

Have you ever been too proud to ask God if He wants to teach you anything? Has your arguing with God stepped across the line of rightful reverence and become instead taunting mockery?

Elihu may be putting his finger on a sore spot for many of us!

Who was the guilty? Who brought this upon
    Thee? . . .
'Twas I, Lord Jesus,
I it was denied Thee; I crucified Thee.'
                    — Johann Heermann (translated by Robert Bridges)

Can My Behavior Affect God?

If you sin, that does no harm to God.
If you do wrong many times, does that affect him?
(35:6)

What about this statement of Elihu's?" I asked my students one morning. "Is it true or false?"

"True," one spoke up quickly. "What we do isn't going to affect God."

Another student agreed.

Then a third spoke up quietly.

"Why, then," she asked them, "was there a Calvary?"

Scene VIII
The Garbage Dump
During a Storm

God

Job: wet, humbled, ready to listen.

Reference: 38:1—42:6.

What is the Book of Job but a scolding poem—
Job scolding God and God scolding Job, Job
hurling questions at God out of the aching,
anguished cage of his finite self, and an infinite,
personal God thundering a reply.

— Edna Hong

Out of the Storm

Thunder announces the approaching storm
(36:33).

As Elihu speaks, the sky darkens. Ominous rumblings of
thunder sound. Lightning rips open the sky. The cattle hud-
dle together, heads down, tails facing into the wind. Rabbits
scamper hurriedly to the deep woods. Birds flutter anx-
iously, twittering and chattering excitedly. Stillness hovers
over the land. Dark clouds race in from the west and black
out the sun.

Then lightning zigzags across the blackness and bathes
the landscape in eerie whiteness. The thunder swells in vol-
ume, its reverberations shaking the earth. And then the
heavens open, and the rain pours down. Tall trees bend,
their branches sweeping and swishing the rain as it falls in
sheets.

Job crouches on the ground. He grasps at his sackcloth,
trying to pull it over his head to shield his body from the
driving rain. Lightning blazes again. There is a sharp crack,
then another sudden clap of thunder. Under his sackcloth,
Job breathes heavily. Fear and despair clutch him. Even the

brutal, uncontrollable forces of nature have turned against him now. Job cries weakly.

And then suddenly, the storm is over. The writer describes what follows.

> And now the light in the sky is dazzling, too bright for us to look at it; and the sky has been swept clean by the wind. A golden glow is seen in the north, and the glory of God fills us with awe (37:21, 22).

God is about to speak.

The only right attitude towards suffering is worship or humble self-surrender. This is not a grovelling humiliation but a sober humility. This is not to commit intellectual and moral suicide; this is to acknowledge the limits of our finite minds. This is, in a word, to let God be God and to be content to be ourselves, to remain mere humans.

— J. R. W. Stott

Mere Humans

Then out of the storm the Lord spoke to Job (38:1).

Drenched and clutching his dripping sackcloth, still shaking from the stupendous crashes of thunder and the brilliant blazes of lightning, Job crouches on the ground and hears a voice.

"Who are you . . . ?"

Job trembles.

"Who are you to question my wisdom with your ignorant, empty words?" (38:2).

Job covers his face with his hands and begins to rock back and forth, whimpering softly.

"Stand up now like a man and answer the questions I ask you" (38:3).

What a bracing command!

"Enough groveling in the mud, Job," God is saying. "Enough commiserating over you and your sad state. Enough boasting. Enough of your presuming to put Me on a level with you. Enough back-talking to Me. Enough asking Me to arrange things as you wish. Enough questioning My power to keep things under control. Enough questioning My wisdom in letting happen what happens. Enough of your name-calling and your accusations. Stand up now like a man! I have some questions to ask you."

Job puts the palms of his skinny arms flat on the muddy ground and pushes himself to his feet. Dripping wet, he stands before God.

And now the questions begin. In a magnificent discourse, God portrays for Job the awesomeness and immensity of the universe (38:4—39:30).

"Were you there when I made the world?" God asks. "If you know so much, tell me about it."

"Who closed the gates to hold back the sea?"

"Job, have you ever in all your life commanded a day to dawn?"

"Have you been to the springs in the depths of the sea?"

"Has anyone ever shown you the gates that guard the dark world of the dead?"

"Can you tie the Pleiades together or loosen the bonds that hold Orion?"

"Do you know the laws that govern the skies, and can you make them apply to earth?"

"Can you shout orders to the clouds and make them drench you with rain?"

On and on the questions come.

Job covers his face with his hands.

God is relentless. He says, in effect, "Job, if you have to trust Me for running the world, can you not trust Me with the small details of your life?"

Then, probably with infinite tenderness in His voice, God asks, "Job, you challenged Almighty God. Will you give up now, or will you answer?" (40:1, 2).

Job can't raise his head. His words are few. His voice is low, so low we hardly can catch the words.

"I spoke foolishly, Lord. What can I answer?" He hesitates. "I will not try to say anything else. I have already said more than I should" (40:3-5).

Something has happened to Job. The wonder of God has gripped him. Morning is breaking. As Dostoevski expressed it, no longer will he believe as a child. The hosannas that shall soon escape his lips have been born, as they have for many of us, in a furnace of doubt.

Wonder is central to faith's venture.
Wonder involves arrest, apprehension, and
complete capture,
leading to recognition and then to capitulation.
— Gerhard E. Frost

Morning Is Breaking

Stand up now like a man, and answer my questions (40:7).

God does not let us off easily. He often seems to have yet more questions to ask.

"Are you trying to prove that I am unjust—to put me in the wrong and yourself in the right?" (40:8).

Job is squirming. He is wishing he hadn't said all the things he had.

"Are you as strong as I am? . . . If so, stand up in your honor and pride" (40:9, 10).

"I'll give you a test case," God says, in effect. "Consider the proud and wicked. If you can bring them under control so we have social justice and streets safe to walk day and night, ah, then I'll be the first to praise you and admit that you won the victory yourself."

Job's chin is on his chest. His damp, frizzled hair falls over his face.

A strange little lesson in zoology follows, in which the mighty creatures of that day are described. The full significance of this discourse remains a mystery—at least to me.

At last God is silent. He waits for Job to reply, the same way He does with us when we've heard His Word. Will we now be "doers," or only "hearers"?

Job's words are few, eloquent in their simplicity.

"I know, Lord, that you are all-powerful; that you can do everything you want. You ask how I dare question your wisdom when I am so very ignorant" (42:2, 3).

Oh, Job. What different words you utter now!

"I talked about things I did not understand, about marvels too great for me to know" (42:3).

It is as though Job is saying, "I can accept it now, God, that there are some mysteries that perhaps I shall never understand. And that is as it should be. I had forgotten who You are. I was bringing You down to my human level, trying to talk to You as to another human. I forgot, Lord. Of course I cannot hope to understand all. If I were to understand all" (and perhaps his head is tilted back now, his eyes aglow with worship and wonder), "You wouldn't be my God. How foolish I have been!"

"You told me to listen while you spoke," he continues, "and to try to answer your questions" (42:4).

He pauses, then goes on.

"Then [that is, back in the midst of my trouble when I was arguing with my friends and with You] I knew only what others had told me." He pauses and looks again at his Lord. "But now I have seen you with my own eyes" (42:5). He hesitates. His voice breaks. He sinks to the ground at the feet of his God. "So I am ashamed of all I have said," he sobs broken-heartedly, "and repent in dust and ashes" (42:6).

And as God stoops to lift up this broken but healed man, the curtain is drawn.

For Job, the long, anguished time of trial is over. The rebellion of his heart is stilled. The anger has drained away. He had thought his God absent, and this imagined absence was Job's keenest suffering. But now he experiences God's presence again, more real than ever.

Out of the ashes of suffering a new relationship between Job and his God is being born. So familiar did Job feel with his God before that he argued with Him, harangued, scolded, and accused Him as a person would a fellow human being. But out of the blinding light following the storm, when God spoke to Job, it was not as a man talks to his equal, but as the Creator talks to the created. And a new relationship is born.

"What is true of the relation between two men," Kierkegaard writes in *The Journals*, "is not true of the relation of man to God; that the longer they live together and the better they get to know each other, the closer do they come to one another. The very opposite is true in relation to God. The longer one lives with Him, the more infinite He becomes—and the smaller one becomes oneself."

Job has found his place before his God and is at peace. The writer of the Book of Hebrews promises us a similar rest from our struggle, too, if we will but trust in Jesus Christ.

The deep sense of humility Job feels now is cleansing and ennobling. Job will be able to walk taller than ever, even though he carries a humble heart within his breast now. The painful memories will still linger. But they will be sweetened by God's arms around him, God's wiping away his tears, God's voice assuring him that one day he will understand fully. And wonder of wonders, the God who loves in this way is an infinite God who loves finite man.

Job shakes his head in wonder. Morning is breaking for him. I think I hear him saying, "Love so amazing, so divine," shall freely have "my soul, my life, my all."

If God continually revealed himself to us, faith could have no value, as we could not help believing. And if he never revealed himself, there could hardly be such a thing as faith.

— Blaise Pascal

The Lord Did Answer

The Lord did answer. He will answer. Job's cries have not been in vain. The Lord is not dull of hearing.

Nor is His heart hardened. He will respond.

How can we be sure of this? "He who did not spare his own Son but gave him up for us all, will he not also give us all things with him?" (Rom. 8:32, RSV).

As E. Stanley Jones has explained, because God loves us and because He grieves that sin has separated us from Him, a cross has lain on His heart since the time His creatures chose to be gods unto themselves. But if God is an eternal Spirit, how were humans going to know about this cross? How were humans going to know God grieves and cares? A spirit is not visible to the eyes of earth-creatures.

Only as God was willing to take human form, and innocently die a physical death that many could witness, would people for all time know of that cross. So God took that step. The death of His eternal Son is an historical fact. And if God was willing to go to these lengths to portray clearly for us His heart of love—and even more profoundly, to bear for us all the awful consequences of our sin and become sin for us (who can understand this?)—can we not believe He will continue to meet our needs and answer when we call?

"Then the Lord answered Job." God has answered us. He will continue to do so.

A saint's life is in the hands of God like a bow and arrow in the hands of an archer. God is aiming at something the saint cannot see. He stretches and strains, and the saint cries, "I cannot stand any more!" God does not heed. He goes on stretching until his purpose is in sight. Then he lets fly.

— Oswald Chambers

Then . . .

Then . . . the Lord spoke to Job (38:1).

Then—in God's timing, when Job had failed to receive help from his friends and was still left with upsetting questions.

Then—when the voices of all others were stilled.

Then—not in quietness, but in the whistling of a whirlwind God spoke.

Then—when denying his sinful state and waxing bold in boasting, Job was about to miss out on God's salvation.

Then—in God's time deliverance came.

In the fullness of time God also sent His Son. At the right time.

Then—when non-Jewish people were turning from the dying Greek gods yet seeking meaning for life.

Then—when Rome, with her network of roads had made distant places more easily accessible so the Good News could be carried far and wide.

Then—when relatively peaceful conditions existed.

Then—when a common language was being spoken.

Then God sent His Son.

194

Then—in God's time deliverance comes.

Two sisters from Bethany sent word to Jesus that their brother was ill. Jesus waited until Lazarus had died. Two remarkable facts are recorded: "Now Jesus *loved* Martha and her sister and Lazarus. So when he heard that he [Lazarus] was ill, he stayed two days longer in the place where he was. *Then* after this he said to the disciples, 'Let us go into Judaea again' " (John 11:5-7, RSV, italics mine.)

Jesus loved them, so He delayed coming to their rescue. *Then*, after He knew Lazarus was dead and all human hope smashed, *then* He went to them.

God's timing. Do you believe in it? When He seemingly is deaf to our cries and doesn't come to our rescue, can we still believe He is then in control? That He is listening and has heard? That in *His* time He will come with deliverance?

I sought the Lord, and afterward I knew
He moved my soul to seek Him, seeking me;
It was not I that found, O Savior true;
No, I was found of Thee.

— The Pilgrim Hymnal (1904)

When God Becomes Real to Us

Then I knew only what others had told me, but
now I have seen you with my own eyes (42:5).

My mother did her best to become real to her grandchildren during the years we lived in Africa. We had left, Luverne with two-year-old Dan on his arm and I holding one-year-old Judy. Although they had known Grandma before we left, memories of her soon misted away. And Janet and David, who were born in Africa, had never seen her.

But Grandma loved her unseen grandchildren. Weekly she wrote to them. She sent pictures, which we put up in the children's rooms. At Christmas and on birthdays she sent gifts. She recorded stories and poems on tapes, and she sat at the piano and played and sang to them. Grandma frequently crept into our conversations, and we prayed for her daily.

Furlough time came. We went home to the States with children ages seven, six, four, and two. Home to Grandma's house. And there the children gazed into her face, finely etched with the joys and cares of many years. They felt her

196

arms around them and the velvet caress of lips softened with age. Her love filtered through, and though she had been there all along, now she became real to them.

This was what Job was describing when, at the end of his long tortured testing, he cried out: "Then I know only what others had told me, but now I have seen you with my own eyes."

A day came too for me, many years ago, when I exclaimed with awe and joy, "Before I knew only what others had told me, but now . . ." Before, I knew only what others had told me of how God would adopt me as His child. I learned He cared for me because He daily gives me gifts, and most important of all, because He gave His only Son to die for me. Many assured me I could trust Him, for He had proven faithful to them. I heard many, many more things about God from others.

The picture of His Son hung in our home. His name frequently crept into our conversation. Almost daily, we prayed to Him. Then one day He became as real to me as my father and mother. What led to this?

First, I needed to see myself as completely and utterly lost if God did not step in and rescue me. To glimpse this dark side of me shook me, because for years, in order to be God's person I had been trying very hard to "be as good as I could." It shattered me to discover what I was really like. Weeping, I cried out, "Oh, Lord, I deserve hell; I really do!"

Then, into that vacuum of complete helplessness and immense need, Jesus came to me. With outstretched hands He offered me Himself, and forgiveness, and a new heart, and His Spirit to indwell me.

It seemed too good to be true, that I could come to Him just as I was, with all my sin. But when I did, the miracle took place. The Holy Spirit assured me I was forgiven. And the Lord Jesus became amazingly real to me and very precious. I felt His love. I was conscious of His presence. My

197

heart burned while a new indescribable peace pooled within.

What had happened to Job had happened to me. After Job's four friends, with their poor theology and wrong approaches, had tried in vain to comfort Job, God Himself spoke to Job out of a whirlwind. Catching that glimpse of God and His greatness and majesty left Job humble, submissive, repentant, and fumbling for words. But Job also was enabled to believe and trust even though all his questions were not answered. And this change took place because God revealed Himself to Job. It was God's work. God's initiative. And Job's response.

Hearing about God from others was good and most needful. But getting personally acquainted with Him came as a result of His revealing Himself to me. I saw my need. I cried to Him to save me, to help me believe. And as I cried, I experienced what Martin Luther, in his catechism, described to be the work of the Holy Spirit: "I believe I cannot by my own reason or strength believe in Jesus Christ, my Lord, or come to Him. But the Holy Spirit has called me through the gospel, enlightened me with His gifts, and sanctifies me in the true faith." Amen, Lord! I cry. This is true!

Whenever God gives a vision to a saint, he puts him, as it were, in the shadow of his hand, and the saint's duty is to be still and listen.

— Oswald Chambers

Sometimes When the Curtain Is Drawn . . .

After the Lord had finished speaking to Job . . . (42:7).

I wonder what the Lord said to His servant Job after the curtain was drawn. What went on between those two in private?

It reminds me of the encounter Jesus had with Zacchaeus. After a casual conversation in which Jesus expressed His wish to visit with Zacchaeus in his home, we find Zacchaeus some time later crying out to the Lord, "If I have defrauded anyone of anything, I restore it fourfold" (Luke 19:8, RSV). What caused that confession, that resolve, I have wondered? What had Jesus said to Zacchaeus?

And what did God say to Job when He lifted him up? There are moments when God speaks to each of us alone, moments that are so holy that the curtain must be drawn over them.

Let us not hurry away from those intimate times. Let us linger long enough to be sure the Lord has finished speaking to us. For if we do, like Job, we shall emerge changed people.

No one could tell me where my soul might be
I sought for God, but God eluded me.
I sought my brother out and found all three
My soul, my God, and all humanity.

Healing . . .
As We Reach Out

It would seem as though the turning point for Job came as
the result of the sudden dramatic encounter with the Lord
in the storm. For many of us, however, recovery is a slow,
almost imperceptible recovery over a long period of time,
until finally one day we discover we are feeling better, and
the hurt is not quite as grievous, and yes, if it is permissible
to say so, we are even happy.

My own recovery from grief came slowly. I suppose
what helped more than anything else to bring healing was
the welcoming into our home of a little boy and a baby girl,
followed by the birth of two more children during our years
in East Africa.

Joe Bayly, who has buried three children, states that
what seemed to help his wife and him most was taking into
their home a number of hurting people who needed tender,
loving care. For Carole Hanson, the wife of a Vietnam-era
POW, it was active leadership in the POW/MIA movement.

Anything that coaxes us outside our own miseries
seems to help. It is more blessed to give than to receive.

But whatever is effective in bringing healing to us, for
most of us it will be a slow process, like the gradual dawning

of a new day. Healing is most effective when it includes for us, as it did for Job, a fresh encounter with our living Lord. But we must also remember that our Lord sometimes comes to us hidden and disguised in the persons of those who need to receive His love through us.

Scene IX
Job's New Home

God

Eliphaz, Bildad, Zophar

Job's seven sons and three daughters

A host of relatives and friends

Reference: 42:7-16.

This is the essence of true guilt, that in the face of
the revelation of God and his activity, we refuse
God and we prefer death to life, slavery to
freedom, and enmity to reconciliation.

— Eric Wahlstrom

False Guilt

The Lord . . . said to Eliphaz, "I am angry with
you and your two friends, because you did not
speak the truth about me" (42:7).

Extraordinary turnabout of events! The scolders become
the scolded!

Edna Hong, in her book *The Downward Ascent*, writes
that there are three kinds of false guilt.

(1) The false guilt of being a brought-up or born-again
Christian and yet not being as perfect as you think a
brought-up or born-again Christian ought to be. (2)
The false guilt of having secret doubts about God and
your Christian faith. (3) The false guilt for being angry
with God, sometimes even hating him.

Job's friends laid all three kinds heavily on him. By
doing so, they unwittingly sought to move him from a position of grace to one of self-righteous striving for some
intangible perfection, which would be evident by Job's not
having any more troubles!

Hong asserts that this "laying upon others the burden
of a new law, a law requiring them to prove to the world

their instant sanctification, their instant sainthood" is the source of real guilt, guilt that stems from offending God.

This is why God is angry with Job's friends. This is why God tells Job to pray for them. Smug, self-assured, and oh, so holy! They need to be forgiven.

Peacemaking proceeds by letting the past pass,
And being present with and supportive of
the other in the here and now.

— David W. Augsburger

Praying for Those Who Hurt Me

"Job will pray for you. . . ." Then, after Job had
prayed for his three friends . . . (42:8, 10).

Any ill feeling or resentment Job might harbor toward his
friends must not mar the new purified relationship between
Job and God. So God asks Job to pray for his friends. And
Job does.

It is impossible to continue to pray for a person and
not be changed. Feelings toward that person change. If there
has been ill will, concern and love will slowly melt the hate
and take over.

Of course, it is never easy to begin. J. B. Phillips suggests we must be honest with God about our feelings and
begin by confessing: "I hate the sight of so-and-so. He (she)
irritates me beyond endurance and always brings out the
worst in me. Help me to pray for him (her)."

It takes humility to launch out on such an adventure.
But if we do, the situation invariably will improve. At least
our hearts' attitudes will be changed. And this is of supreme
importance, for nothing must be allowed to cloud our trans-
parent relationship with our God, and bitterness toward

others quickly produces fog. So Job must pray for those who hurt him.

This must be why Jesus taught, "Love your enemies and pray for those who persecute you" (Matt. 5:44).

              . . . not a perfect saint
              . . . simply one of God's patients, not yet cured
              . . . not only tears to be dried but stains to be
                  scoured.
                                                    — C. S. Lewis

Job's Daughters

> The Lord blessed the last part of Job's life even
> more than he had blessed the first. . . . He was
> the father of seven sons and three daughters. He
> called the oldest daughter Jemimah, the second
> Keziah, and the youngest Keren Happuch. There
> were no other women in the whole world as beau-
> tiful as Job's daughters. Their father gave them a
> share of the inheritance along with their brothers
> (42:12-15).

Extraordinary indeed is the prominence given to Job's
daughters in the closing lines of this grand story. Only the
daughters are named. Their beauty is extolled. And, wonder
of wonders, they are given an inheritance along with their
brothers. How could this be? How could Job consider these
girls of equal value with his sons, when his contemporaries
thanked God every morning that they were not born
women?

Could it be that Job, the rebel against the trite, pat
religious answers of his day, was also Job the rebel when
it came to accepting the bias toward women so common in
his day?

At the same time, Job's concern for women seems a bit confused. Expecting his wife to bear 20 children was presumptuous, indeed!

Oh, dear! How human Job is. Just like us. Strong in some areas. Blind in others.

Love . . . so that you may be sons of your Father
who is in heaven; for he makes his sun rise on the
evil and on the good, and sends rain on the just
and on the unjust.

— Matthew 5:44, 45, RSV

Why Is God So Good to Me?

The Lord made him [Job] prosperous again and
gave him twice as much as he had had before. . . .
The Lord blessed the last part of Job's life even
more than he had blessed the first (Job 42:10,
12).

We were all sitting around a campfire, a group of us.
Among us was Al, short of stature, square-shouldered,
squinting with one eye, rugged, and down-to-earth. He had
lived a rather ordinary life, as most of us have—a life sprin-
kled with trouble and success, joy and sorrow.

We were sharing answers to the question, "When we
see our Lord face to face, what questions will we ask Him?"

When Al's turn came, he said simply, "I'm going to ask
Him, 'Why have you been so good to me, Lord?' "

I wonder if this was the question that escaped Job's
lips at the end of his life, after the Lord had prospered him
more than ever. Some have asked if the significance of Job's
testing wasn't lost when, in the end, he prospered more
than ever.

210

From a human point of view, perhaps. But this is God's way, acting in grace. Our generous, extravagant God pours out His blessings not because we deserve them or earn them—we never do—but simply because He is love.

Love can never be satisfied with just saying in words, "I love you." Love must give gifts as well—visible tokens. Our God is love, and so He gives and gives and gives, and Job, at the end of his life, winds up more prosperous than ever.

Skies will grow darker yet but those signed with
the cross of Christ go gaily in the dark.

— G. K. Chesterton

Looking Back

The Book of Job is the story of a man who struggled
through a grief experience.

The book also relates the techniques of his well-meaning but misguided friends as they sought to comfort him
(although in reality they were seeking to control him): techniques of insidious insinuation, direct attacks and accusations, threats, and offering of rewards. We recognize Job's
strength as he withstood the pressure his friends brought to
bear on him and determined to be true to his own understanding of what was right and wrong.

But the Book of Job is more. It is the account of a man
who, because of immense tragedy, thought he had lost his
God forever, and then discovered that God had been with
him all the time.

It is also the story of a man who learned to trust God
without receiving all the answers. For in the end, Job was
never let in on what we have known from the beginning of
this drama—the reason behind all the catastrophes. God
never told Job it was a fiery testing to see if Job would
emerge still trusting Him. Job did emerge with his faith and
trust in God stronger than ever. That was enough. Job had
to learn to trust without receiving answers.

And that is the meaning of faith. Faith is only faith when
we cannot "see" or "understand" but we believe and trust
anyway.

And only when our faith has been tested can we know it is real and not just imagined. "Doctrine without experience," Oscar Blackwelder asserts, "is truth without confirmation."

Job's testing was so severe and costly that it made him reel. We too will stagger. The testing may even knock us for a while. But then, when we lay exhausted and helpless, we discover afresh the depths of rebellion and proud independence that lurk deep within us, and the devilish way we deceive ourselves into believing we are something we really are not.

The only way out is for God to come to our rescue. There must be a fresh, personal encounter with Him which we cannot command, but which God is only too willing to initiate. Through that encounter we, like Job, will rediscover our identity and God's. Humbly, but with relief, we shall acknowledge ourselves to be mere humans in need of Him. We bow before our God as we see Him in His holiness, righteousness, power, and majesty. And I think I hear Job, as he kneels together with me, whispering:

"Oh, how I fear thee, living God
        with deepest, tenderest fears,
And worship thee with trembling hope
        and penitential tears."

That is the way I feel. It is not so much that I have learned a lesson. Rather, I think, it is that my testing has changed me, has made me into someone I was not before.

The Book of Job is also—for me—the account of the journey again to the cross. For when I have fought God, been angry with Him, accused and attacked Him, He himself will come at last and reveal Himself to me afresh—on the cross. For me the cross of Jesus Christ portrays the horrible price God had to pay to set me free from my sin.

The cross, I am convinced, is not a place you and I visit only once.

Job's understanding of a Mediator and Savior was hazy. But Job was stirred profoundly and changed by a revelation of the Creator-Sustainer-God, a revelation many of us lack today. Blessed and sturdy are those Christians to whom the Holy Spirit unveils both revelations: the Mediator on the cross, and the all-powerful God of creation. For the feeling of security that is born in our hearts when we see portrayed on the cross God's immense love for us will become even stronger when we realize that that same God is the One who holds us and all the events of our lives in His hand.

Yet more. He holds history in His hand, and one day He will bring history to a close. But until then, no matter how forbidding the future may appear, our hearts can be at rest. The Creator God, the Redeemer God, is in control. In this faith we rest.

Suggested Reading

For scarred pilgrims who are ever searching for deeper understanding, the author suggests for further reading the following books which have helped her.

Through the Valley of the Kwai, Ernest Gordon, Harper and Bros., New York.

A Grief Observed, C. S. Lewis, a Bantam Book, New York.

Why Do Christians Break Down? William A. Miller, Augsburg Publishing House, Minneapolis, Minn.

Man's Search for Meaning, Viktor E. Frankl, Washington Square Press, New York.

When Going to Pieces Holds You Together, William A. Miller, Augsburg Publishing House, Minneapolis, Minn.

The Valley of the Shadow, Hanns Lilje, Muhlenberg Press, Philadelphia, Pa.

The Cost of Discipleship, Dietrich Bonhoeffer, Macmillan Publishing Co., Inc., New York.

Ministering to Deeply Troubled People, Ernest E. Bruder, Fortress Press, Philadelphia, Pa.

For This Day, J. B. Phillips, Word, Waco, Tex.

Small Man of Nanataki, Liam Nolan, E. P. Dutton & Co., New York.

The Love of God, Oswald Chambers, Christian Literature Crusade, Fort Washington, Pa.

A Serious Call to a Devout and Holy Life, William Law, Baker Book House, Grand Rapids, Mich.

Diary of an Old Soul, George Macdonald, Augsburg Publishing House, Minneapolis, Minn.

My Utmost for His Highest, Oswald Chambers, Dodd, Mead & Company, New York.

The Color of the Night, Gerhard E. Frost, Augsburg Publishing House, Minneapolis, Minn.

The Downward Ascent, Edna Hong, Augsburg Publishing House, Minneapolis, Minn.

Prayers, Michel Quoist, Sheed and Ward, New York.

A Prisoner and Yet, Corrie Ten Boom, Christian Literature Crusade, London.

Good Grief, Granger Westberg, Fortress Press, Philadephia, Pa.